KILLER COUPLES

KILLER COUPLES

DEADLY DUOS AND THEIR HORRIFYING DEEDS

CHARLOTTE GREIG, JOHN MARLOWE
AND PAUL ROLAND

Charlotte Greig graduated with an MA in Intellectual History and started freelancing as a writer and editor for a variety of magazines and newspapers, including NME and the Guardian. She has written a number of books including *Evil Serial Killers* and *The World's Worst Criminals*.

John Marlowe has written widely on true crime and is the author of such titles as *The World's Most Evil Psychopaths*, *Chambers of Horror* and *Evil Women*.

Paul Roland is the author of more than thirty books, including *Investigating the Unexplained*, *The Crimes of Jack the Ripper*, *Life After the Third Reich* and *The Nuremberg Trials*. He has been a freelance feature writer and reviewer for many UK publications such as the *Mail on Sunday*, *Kerrang* and *Total Film*.

This edition published in 2025 by Arcturus Publishing Limited
26/27 Bickels Yard, 151–153 Bermondsey Street,
London SE1 3HA

AD011612UK
Supplier 40, Date 1025, PI00011598

Printed in the UK

Authorised Representative:
Easy Access System Europe - Mustamäe tee 50, 10621 Tallinn, Estonia
gpsr.requests@easproject.com

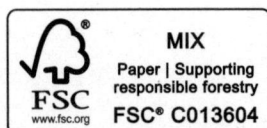

CONTENTS

INTRODUCTION

Serial murder is for the most part a lonely business, a sickness dreamed up in the depths of an isolated, damaged soul. The stereotype of the serial killer is a crazed loner operating in the shadows, so it is peculiarly disturbing to encounter serial killers who act as a team, who have managed to find others to share in their perversion. While there are instances of serial killer teams being simply friends (Kenneth Bianchi and Angelo Buono, or Leonard Lake and Charles Ng, for instance), the most common type of team killers is a pair of lovers. It is appalling to contemplate a kind of love so perverse that it leads couples to share in murder for their own sexual gratification.

Take, for example, the case of Douglas Clark and Carol Bundy. While we can imagine that a man like Clark might be drawn to rape and murder, it almost defies belief that he could bring home the severed head of one of his victims and that his lover, Carol Bundy, could first apply make-up to the dead woman's face and then look on approvingly as Clark committed an act of necrophilia with the head.

Less bizarre, but perhaps even more shocking, is the case of Paul Bernardo and Karla Homolka, in which Homolka deliberately drugged her own 15-year-old sister so that Bernardo could rape her; or that of British killers Ian Brady and Myra Hindley, in which Hindley would lure young girls into Brady's clutches, then take part in torturing them before Brady murdered them.

Sometimes partners are roped in when their lovers need an accomplice to help them kidnap, abuse or murder their victims. And sometimes they become active participants in the crimes and willingly join in when the killing spree begins. These deadly duos have been responsible for an astonishing array of hideous crimes.

Serial killers, typically, are individuals motivated by violent sexual drives that are difficult for most people to understand. Robbery may be an integral part of the killer's pattern of attacks, but it is seldom the only motivation for serial murder. Very few serial killers are motivated purely by financial gain. It seems that, although greed may cause individuals to kill once or twice, on the whole it does not provoke a series of brutal murders. However, there are exceptions to this rule. In some cases, there appears to be no sexual motivation whatsoever on the part of the killer; he or she kills, callously and brutally, to rob the victims of their possessions. These are the gold diggers, criminals who are prepared to murder over and over for no reason other than money – and often surprisingly small amounts of money at that.

Take Faye and Ray Copeland, an elderly couple of Nebraska farmers who murdered transient farm labourers for paltry profits. Likewise, Raymond Fernandez and Martha Beck, another couple who were prepared to kill as part of what were otherwise a series of low-level scams. Even Charles Sobhraj, a man often portrayed as a kind of evil genius among serial killers, mostly murdered backpackers for little more than a passport and a handful of traveller's cheques.

The relatively insignificant gains that these killers make in terms of money and goods point to the fact that they are, in general, true psychopaths: criminals for whom the suffering of others is meaningless. For them, human life is cheap, so much so that they are able to kill again and again without any sign of conscience.

It is this perversion of love – and in particular the reverse of what we conventionally see as the civilizing influence of the woman – that makes the disturbing stories of these demon lovers so profoundly unsettling.

Most of us will never know what destructive potential we possess, but in the following pages you will meet numerous individuals who have committed multiple murders and subjected their victims to unimaginable suffering, and yet have expressed no regret or remorse. The sensation-seeking media call such people 'evil' and demonize them as 'monsters' in a desperate effort to distance them from law-abiding members of society.

But the unpalatable truth is that sexual predators, serial killers and sadists are deceptively ordinary people – on the surface at least. They are not clinically insane, although it would be easier for us to 'understand' their aberrant behaviour if they were. A person of unsound mind will act irrationally and will disregard the risks of getting caught when committing a criminal act. But even the most depraved sex offenders exercise some degree of control over their desires, selecting their victims because of their vulnerability rather than their physical attractiveness. Such people do not act on impulse, even though they often claim that they are overcome by their desires when they see a potential victim. They will have brooded on their crime for days, weeks or even months. But at some point they realize that their fantasy no longer satisfies them, so they take the opportunity to make it a reality. All multiple murderers and serial sex killers are predators and they hunt using their intellect as much as their instincts.

Sadistic serial killers are frequently well organized and well prepared. Many of them use a customized vehicle for the abduction of their victims and they often have a secluded base where they can hold them for as long as they serve their purpose. These are not the actions of an insane person. Even the most depraved killers will attempt to evade detection, which proves that they are capable of reasoning and are therefore legally responsible for their actions.

To divert suspicion they might cultivate an air of respectability by leading an ordered life and holding down a regular job, which is not the act of a person of unsound mind. Such offenders are abnormal, not insane.

It also needs to be acknowledged that sexual desire is not always the motive behind the crimes of serial sex offenders and sadistic killers. In many cases rape and torture are expressions of deep-seated anger. These disturbed individuals have a need to manipulate, dominate and control their victims.

But are these people born evil or has cruelty been instilled in them at an impressionable age? The prevailing theory is that many serious offenders were desensitized to suffering through years of abuse and neglect in their childhood. But while other abuse victims internalize their anguish, sexual predators, sadists or serial killers will externalize it. They derive pleasure from watching others suffer as they did and they get a kick out of being in control. The threat to society is doubled when an aggressive psychotic teams up with a passive-aggressive individual who has internalized their anger. This suppressed rage then finds an outlet when their evil twin reinforces their warped view of the world.

Beware, these killings are not for the faint-hearted.

WILLIAM BURKE AND WILLIAM HARE

I n early 19th-century Edinburgh even the dead did not rest easy. No sooner were corpses interred in the city's cemeteries than they were likely to be dug up in the dead of night by 'resurrectionists' – grave robbers who profited from selling cadavers to the local medical schools.

The golden age of scientific discovery was dawning and the Scottish capital's surgeons were keen to supply their eager students with suitable specimens. However, they were forbidden to do so by an antiquated law which supported the Church's assertion that the act of dissection condemned the soul of the deceased to eternal damnation. It was said that only those whose bodies were intact would enter the kingdom of heaven on the Day of Judgment. As a consequence anatomists were forced to limit their examinations to the corpses of executed criminals and vagrants.

Contrary to popular belief, comparatively few criminals were executed at the turn of the century. Instead, transportation to the colonies had become the preferred punishment for all crimes apart from treason and murder, so fresh specimens from the scaffold were in short supply. Consequently, the only question asked of those selling cadavers was, 'Can you obtain another?' And if so, the fresher the better.

As the grisly trade increased, grieving relatives were forced to consider paying for the installation of 'mort safes' – iron, cage-like contraptions built over and around the graves of the newly deceased, for fear they might be disinterred at dead of night. But few could afford such measures.

While the more enlightened medical men lobbied unsuccessfully for a change in the law, two of their fellow citizens forced the issue by murdering at least 17 people, often their neighbours, in order to procure fresh cadavers. Ironically, neither of Britain's most notorious bodysnatchers personally robbed a grave during their brief criminal careers. They were either too frightened or too workshy to dirty their hands in the kirkyard.

At the time of the murders, which took place between November 1827 and October of the following year, itinerant Irish immigrant William Burke was 36 years old. He considered himself ill-used by society, with no prospect of finding gainful employment and no will to look for it. After abandoning his wife and two children in County Mayo, he emigrated to Scotland where he drifted aimlessly through a succession of labouring jobs. He ended up in Edinburgh where he settled down with Helen (Nell) McDougal, whom he had met while lodging at her home in Maddiston. Helen left her two children and her common-law husband to travel with Burke, who was said to be crudely handsome but sullen and quick-tempered. The couple found cheap lodgings in Tanner's Close in the West Port, a rat run of squalid tenements, gaslit streets and ale houses, where the inhabitants could drink themselves senseless for a shilling.

A Frightful Scheme

With no work, and no hope of finding any, Burke reluctantly endured the company of his landlord, fellow Irish immigrant William Hare, who was generous with his rental income. Hare would buy drinks for anyone who would listen to his idle boasts and his plans to get rich without doing a day's honest work. Little is known of Hare's background, but according to contemporary accounts he was a repulsive, vindictive man who was given to fits of idiotic laughter, when his reptilian features would distort into a hideous mask, giving the impression of a fairground freak. Burke tolerated him so long as he bought the drinks, but he also half hoped that one of Hare's mad schemes might one day make them both rich. In the winter of 1827 they hit on a scheme that promised to do just that.

One of Hare's lodgers, an elderly soldier named Donald, had died suddenly after a long illness. While waiting for the body to be collected, Hare complained long and bitterly to Burke. The old man's rent remained unpaid and there were no known relatives that could be badgered into settling the account. Then it occurred to him that the medical colleges would pay for the corpse, perhaps even more than he was owed. They would split the money equally and be rich men by nightfall. No one would miss the old man or enquire into the cause of his death and there was no risk of being caught – but they would have to act quickly. So they swiftly removed the body from its coffin, hid it elsewhere in the house and replaced it with firewood. After the coffin had been collected they went in search of Professor Munro, the principal anatomist at Edinburgh University Medical School, but by chance they were misdirected to the classrooms of Professor Robert Knox, his colleague. Knox's assistants assured them that they would receive a good price and they were asked to return after dark. When they did so, carrying the still-warm corpse in a sack, Knox's assistants gave them just over £7, more than two weeks' wages for the average skilled labourer.

Mercy Killings

Any fears the two Irishmen might have had were soon dissolved by the keg of whisky they consumed that night. Emboldened by their success and excited by the prospect of more easy money, they were soon looking for their next subject. They did not have long to wait.

A few days later another of Hare's lodgers, Joseph the Miller, fell ill. Although his condition was clearly not life-threatening, Burke and Hare saw no necessity in prolonging the man's agony. They plied him with whisky until he lost consciousness, then one of them pinned his arms and legs down while the other covered his nose and mouth until all signs of life were extinct. Unwittingly, the pair had invented a new method of murder, one which would be named after its creator – 'burking'. It was crude, cruel but foolproof because it left no marks on the body. At first glance it appeared that the victim had died of drink or natural causes.

If Burke and Hare had been careful they could have continued enriching themselves in this way for years. But they drank the wages of sin as soon as they collected them and they also became impatient. They no longer wanted to wait for another ailing lodger to come their way. Instead, they went in search of their victims – those who no one would miss, such as tinkers wandering the cobbled streets and drunks sleeping in doorways.

During the following 11 months Burke and Hare committed 15 more murders without arousing suspicion. Their victims included prostitutes, beggars and the homeless. Many of them had come down to the capital from the Highlands, and from isolated villages, in search of work and so would have no family in Edinburgh to enquire after their whereabouts. One morning, Burke even had the gall to approach a pair of policemen, who were taking an inebriated woman to the police station so that she could sleep off her over-indulgence. He lied that he knew her and offered to take her home. That evening he had another £10 to spend on drink.

By this time several of Dr Knox's students were beginning to talk openly about how their eminent professor was able to offer his class a regular supply of fresh specimens when his colleagues had to make do with a badly decomposed cadaver or, more often, none at all. Their disquiet grew when the body of a local prostitute was delivered to the school. Those who had seen her on the previous day reported that she had looked lively and had been none the worse for drink. But no one dared raise the matter directly with Dr Knox. However, soon afterwards several students voiced their concerns when the body of a well-known local character known as 'Daft Jamie', a youth with a club foot, was placed on the dissecting slab. It was a matter of seconds before they started questioning how this young man had died so suddenly and conveniently within the reach of Burke and Hare, who by now were known to be the sole suppliers of specimens to Dr Knox. The professor confirmed their suspicions by first taking a scalpel to the club foot and then to Jamie's face, in order to eradicate his identifiable features. It was as good as a confession.

And still the students kept silent, fearing scandal and, quite possibly, the closure of the school. Knox, or someone else in authority, may even

William Burke, who was executed in 1829, and William Hare: medical science was hungry for corpses and the two 'bodysnatchers' found a wicked way of supplying these as well as turning a nice little profit for themselves.

have raised the possibility that they might all be named as accomplices if the matter became public.

The Last Victim

On the morning of 29 October 1828, Burke sat drinking his morning draught in the local tavern when he overheard an old woman, Mary Docherty, talking to the barman in a thick Irish accent. He engaged her in conversation and then claimed that he came from the same part of the old country as herself. They might even be related, he told her. With these words he lured Mary back to his house in Tanner's Close, where she met his wife Helen and a couple who were lodging with them, James and Ann Gray. A party was held in order to celebrate the happy chance meeting and the drinking and dancing continued long after the Grays left. They had gone to stay the night with William Hare and his common-law wife Margaret, giving up their room to Mary Docherty just as Burke had hoped. At around midnight another occupant of the house was passing the Burkes' door when he thought he heard two men arguing and a woman's stifled cries of 'Murder!' and 'Get the police!', but when he hurried into the street he could not see a policeman. On returning to the house all was quiet, so he assumed it was a domestic quarrel and he went to bed.

The next morning the Grays returned to Burke's rooms and were surprised to learn that Mary had gone. They were told that she had been turned out of the house in the early hours by Helen, who had claimed that the old woman and her husband were becoming too friendly for comfort. If the Grays found the explanation absurd they did not say so, but their suspicions were aroused when Burke warned Ann not to go near the bed. He later yelled at her when she started towards it to fetch some potatoes stored underneath. As soon as they were alone in the room the Grays looked under the bed and were horrified to see the body of the old woman. As they raced from the house they ran into Helen, who asked them where they were going in such a hurry. James accused her of murder and told her that they were going to fetch the police, which sent her into a panic. She begged them not to do so. Then she offered to share the profits with them if they kept silent, which only infuriated them further. However, by the time the police were summoned the body had vanished. Without it, there were no grounds for arresting William and Helen Burke.

But then a neighbour informed the police that two men had been seen carrying a large tea chest from the house only an hour or so before. When questioned, William claimed that Mrs Docherty had left at 7 o'clock that morning, whereas Helen asserted that the old woman had departed at 7 o'clock that evening. The discrepancy in their stories was sufficient to have them brought in for further questioning. Word soon went around the West Port that murder most foul had been perpetrated at Tanner's Close and someone suggested that the authorities should pay a visit to the dissecting rooms of Dr Knox. There they found a body which was identified by James Gray as being that of Mary Docherty.

By nightfall William Hare and Margaret were also in custody. Their conflicting and inconsistent statements convinced the authorities that they were guilty, but there was no physical evidence and there were no eyewitnesses. All of the evidence was circumstantial. The Lord Advocate believed that most of the guilt lay with Burke, so in order to force the issue and secure a conviction, he offered Hare immunity if he testified against Burke and Helen. Hare seized the chance to save his own skin and he confessed to the crimes, which now included the killing of Daft Jamie and the prostitute Mary Paterson, bringing the total number of victims to 15.

Burke's Trial and Execution

The trial of William Burke began on Christmas Eve 1828, with Helen named as his accomplice in the killing of Mary Docherty. The prosecution case relied almost entirely on the eyewitness testimony of William and Margaret Hare, the statements made by the Grays – which affirmed that the body of an old woman had been hidden in the house but was then spirited away – and the testimony of the lodger who had heard a woman crying 'Murder!' earlier that evening. Helen Burke's solicitor argued that she had been the woman who had cried out in horror when she had witnessed the old woman's death. He went on to say that the fact that she had been seen in the company of several of the victims did not prove that she was implicated in their deaths. It was a poor defence, but it sowed the seed of reasonable doubt.

On Christmas morning the jury returned with its verdicts. Burke was guilty, but the case against Helen was 'not proven', a uniquely Scottish verdict which implied that the accused had escaped imprisonment only because there was insufficient evidence to secure a conviction. On hearing the sentence Burke embraced Helen and wept.

'You are out of the scrape,' he said.

In the following weeks Burke made two formal confessions, which were published in broadsheets and sold by hawkers on the street corners of the city. Damned by his own words and abandoned by his accomplice, William Burke resigned himself to his fate. On 28 January 1829 he was led through the jeering crowds who surged around the scaffold on the Lawnmarket. They called for Hare and Dr Knox to share his fate.

The Aftermath

Remarkably, the eminent anatomist escaped prosecution, but was hounded by stone-throwing crowds at his home and at the medical college. The popularity of his classes dwindled significantly in the weeks and months after the trial. He applied for vacant posts at Edinburgh University Medical School, but he was rejected twice.

Eventually he left for London, where he obtained a position at a cancer hospital. He died in 1862. Although Burke swore that Knox had known nothing of the method by which the corpses were obtained, it seems implausible that a renowned anatomist would not have recognized the signs of a violent – or at least unnatural – death when dissecting the bodies.

The body of William Burke was taken down from the scaffold and delivered to the medical college, where it was dismembered in full view of the students who had attended the dissection of his victims. His skeleton was then put on public display in the college museum, together with his death mask and several items made from his tanned skin. It proved an effective deterrent. The incidence of grave robbing rapidly declined and the practice was all but eradicated by the Anatomy Act of 1832, which permitted the regular supply of dead bodies for dissection.

Hare did not escape justice, however. Angry mobs pursued him and the two women, driving them out of Scotland and harassing them whenever they attempted to settle down. Margaret is thought to have eventually returned to Ireland, it was rumoured that Helen had gone to Australia and William Hare was last heard of in Carlisle. It is not known if there is any truth in the story that he was thrown into a lime pit by an angry mob, forcing him to end his days as a blind beggar on the streets of London.

DR HENRY CLARK AND AUGUSTA FULLAM

India is infested with poisonous snakes, none more deadly than the human variety. Some blame the stifling heat, others the exotic setting for the strange effect the subcontinent had on its white colonial inhabitants in the days of the Raj. Many prim upper-class ladies and starch-collared gentlemen lost their inhibitions when the sun went down. One fatally affected fellow was Dr Henry Clark, who blamed the murder of his wife on the 'thugees', a fanatical cult who worshipped Kali, the eight-armed goddess of death. Dr Clark had a cast-iron alibi, which placed him several miles away at the time of the killing in March 1913 and in full view of several reliable witnesses. But there were rumours that the good doctor had been guilty of conduct unbecoming a gentleman when he had pursued a relationship with a married woman, Mrs Augusta Fullam.

The rumours were well founded because the police found almost 400 letters from Dr Clark to Mrs Fullam when they searched the lady's home in Agra. The letters did not only contain words of love – they also revealed the details of a plot to poison the unsuspecting Mr Fullam. Dr Clark supplied the arsenic powder and Augusta administered it. When her husband complained of stomach cramps he was taken to hospital, where Dr Clark finished him off with a second dose. The thugees, it transpired, had been paid by Dr Clark to remove his wife from the scene so that he could be comforted in his bereavement by the young widow. The couple would then arouse little suspicion when they married. Sadly, the only solemn vows Dr Clark made were to the priest who accompanied him to the gallows on 26 March 1913. Fullam was spared the noose because she was pregnant at the time of her trial, but she was given a life sentence in one of India's most formidable prisons. Mercifully, she died of heatstroke the following year.

GORDON AND SARAH NORTHCOTT

In the late 1920s the citizens of Los Angeles went to the movies several times a week. For the price of a ticket they bought into a fairy-tale world where good always triumphed over evil and every story had a happy ending. So when a local man and his mother were accused of kidnapping and butchering innocent children in their own back yard, the public refused to believe that they could be guilty of such horrific crimes. Even the police preferred to believe that the victims had merely run away from home. They went so far as to commit an innocent mother to a lunatic asylum rather than admit that a boy claiming to be her missing son could be lying in order to escape from his abusive parents.

Digging up the Truth

The whole sickening story began in September 1928 when a Canadian woman, Winnefred Clark, contacted the United States federal authorities to report that her 15-year-old son Sanford had been abducted by his own uncle. The boy had apparently gone to stay with Gordon Stewart Northcott two years earlier with his mother's blessing, but a series of strange letters, supposedly written by the boy, was sufficiently unsettling for Winnefred to send her daughter Jessie to California to investigate. Jessie returned to confirm their worst fears. Gordon was sexually abusing the boy. He had even made an attempted assault on her, but she had fought him off and escaped.

The federal authorities wasted no time in raiding Northcott's poultry farm, only to find that 'Uncle Gordon' and his mother, Sarah Louise, had vanished, leaving the boy to fend for himself. When interviewed, Sanford claimed that he had been forced to witness the rape and murder of other boys and had even participated in their abduction, in order to save his own skin. He could see that the detectives doubted his incredible story so he promised to show them where the bodies were buried. Sure enough, he led them to two hastily dug graves, where human remains were unearthed. Two axes with matted blood and human hair on their blades were also recovered from the site and other body fragments were found scattered elsewhere on the farm. But hampered by primitive forensic techniques, investigators were unable to identify the victims. All they could say for certain was that the remains were those of male children and that they had met a violent end.

Other incriminating items were found elsewhere on the property. There were letters from another abductee and Boy Scout badges belonging to brothers Lewis and Nelson Winslow, who had been kidnapped on their way home in May. However, there was no sign of nine-year-old Walter Collins who had disappeared on his way to a cinema in Lincoln Heights, Los Angeles, on 10 March. Witnesses had reported seeing a boy's dead body wrapped in newspaper on the back seat of a car driven by a 'foreign-looking' couple on that day, but the car's occupants had given their pursuers the slip.

'Try Him Out'

The Los Angeles police force was looking pretty incompetent by now and it needed to show results, but Captain J.J. Jones overstepped the mark by a mile when he attempted to convince distraught Christine Collins that another boy was her son and that she was simply too upset to

Gordon Northcott and his mother Sarah Louise, who perhaps in an effort to gain sympathy also claimed to be his grandmother.

recognize him! Arthur Hutchins had his own reasons for masquerading as the missing child – he had run away from his own hated stepmother – but Jones did not question his story. He continued to insist that Arthur Hutchins was Walter Collins and he accused Christine Collins of denying it in order to embarrass his department. She should take the boy home and 'try him out' for a few weeks, he said, until she came to her senses. Even though the poor woman returned three weeks later with documentary proof that the boy in her care was not Walter – she had brought her son's dental records and sworn statements from several people who had known him – it was not enough. Jones had her committed to a mental institution under a provision that gave senior police officers the power to institutionalize 'troublesome witnesses'.

Handwriting analysis finally exposed Arthur Hutchins' charade and he was reunited with his stepmother. Captain Jones was forced to free Christine Collins, but an apology was not forthcoming.

The Questions Remain

Meanwhile, the killers of Walter Collins had split up in the hope of eluding the police, but they were captured at separate locations in Canada and brought to trial. Under interrogation, Gordon Northcott hinted at having killed nine boys, possibly even 20, but in the event he only confessed to five murders, including the Winslow brothers and Walter Collins. Northcott's mother, Sarah Louise, freely admitted her part in the killings but later stalled for time by denying that she had known the victims.

However, her grandson, young Sanford, whose abduction had uncovered the whole sordid story, told detectives that his grandmother had told him that they would each strike the child with the axe so that they would equally share the guilt. This seems to have been an attempt to frighten Sanford into staying quiet. He was later convicted of having played a minor role in the murders and was sent to a youth offenders' institution for several years.

Gordon attempted to defend himself at his trial in January 1929, but his clumsy efforts to convince the jury of his intellectual superiority only served to alienate them. They became convinced that he was both a sexual sadist and a pathological liar. His mother was no help.

On the stand she claimed to be his grandmother. She told the court a bizarre story of how her husband had raped their daughter Winnefred, who had later given birth to Gordon. If this was intended to elicit the jury's sympathies and explain Gordon's pathology it did not work. By this time the all-male jury could take no more of the defendants' fantasies and they were nauseous from hearing the sickening details of their crimes. They found both defendants guilty. Sarah Louise Northcott was sentenced to life imprisonment and her son Gordon was sentenced to death. He was hanged on 2 October 1930.

In an effort to erase all memory of the crimes the citizens of Wineville petitioned to change the name of their town to Mira Loma. But one person who could not forgive or forget was Christine Collins. She instigated proceedings against the Los Angeles Police Department for false imprisonment. But although she won her case Captain Jones refused to pay her restitution and Jones and his superior, Chief Davis, were reinstated.

Christine managed to get permission to meet face to face with Gordon Northcott before his execution, but he cruelly denied that he had abducted her son and she, incredibly, believed him. She spent the rest of her days searching in vain for the boy who never came home.

BONNIE AND CLYDE

The 'Roaring Twenties' and the early 1930s are remembered as an era of glitzy jazz clubs, flappers, fast cars and gangsters with money to burn and no respect for the law. Big shots like Al Capone had grown fat on the back of the Volstead Act, a universally unpopular law that prohibited the manufacture and sale of alcohol. It had been passed by Congress to appease a vociferous lobby of moral crusaders – religious do-gooders who wanted to save the souls of America's youth, which they feared were being corrupted by the demon drink.

But the new law instead gave rise to an insatiable thirst for illegal liquor and created a new breed of criminal – men who grew so rich by selling bootleg hooch that they could afford to pay corrupt law enforcement officials and politicians to look the other way.

Prohibition was still in force when the Wall Street Crash of 1929 dragged the United States into the Great Depression, thereby ending the 'American Dream' of prosperity and opportunity for all. Overnight, thousands of businesses went bust and millions of workers lost their jobs. Day by day, the queues grew longer at the soup kitchens and 'bread lines', and at the height of the Depression the unemployed camped in Washington's parks to bring their plight to the attention of Capitol Hill. Only the gangsters and the banks remained immune, or so it seemed.

In the rural backwaters of America, many families found themselves impoverished and homeless as the banks foreclosed on farms and businesses with ruthless indifference. Tested to the limits of their endurance, the God-fearing folks of the Great Plains turned to their Christian faith for answers, but it seemed that the good Lord, too, had turned away from them.

In 1930 a terrible drought struck the region with the enormity of a biblical plague, turning the once fertile farmlands into what became known as the Dust Bowl. Huge dust storms stripped the land of its top soil, leaving the plains as uninhabitable as a desert.

Public Enemies

In this climate of despair and and disillusionment more than a few country boys turned to crime – and got away with it, too, so long as they kept within the county boundaries. But as soon as they crossed the state lines their crimes became a federal felony, which gave the FBI the authority to hunt them down. Bank robbers such as John Dillinger, 'Baby Face' Nelson and 'Pretty Boy' Floyd became unlikely folk heroes, stealing from the rich and redistributing their newly acquired wealth to the poor, while leading J. Edgar Hoover and his G-men a merry dance across the states.

Bonnie and Clyde were high-spirited young lovers with no roots, no responsibilities and a fatal belief in their own immortality, so robbing banks while sticking a middle digit up at the authorities must have seemed like a great adventure. Besides, it was the only work that paid a steady wage. They knew that it could all only end in imprisonment or death, but they must have felt that they had nothing to lose. Fate had dealt them loaded dice from the start.

And fate, it seemed, had also had a hand in their meeting. Just before Christmas 1929 Clyde was visiting the sister of a friend in Dallas, who had slipped on the ice and broken her arm. Bonnie was in the kitchen mixing hot chocolate when Clyde walked in to see what all the noise was about. The attraction was instant.

Bonnie Elizabeth Parker (born 1 October 1910 in Rowena, Texas) was petite – she was just under 5 ft (1.52 m) tall – and she had strawberry blonde hair and freckles. But although the local hicks might have found her attractive, she did not possess the qualities that would hook the kind of man who could keep her in the manner to which she wished to become accustomed. She had the brains to get decent grades in high school, but she was painfully aware that she would never amount to anything unless she could force people to sit up and take notice of her. After Bonnie's father died, her mother moved the family to Cement City, where they lived with Bonnie's grandparents. Bonnie soon eloped with local tough guy Roy Thornton, a young man who was as impatient to get rich as she was. But he was stupid enough to get caught and was sentenced to a long stretch in prison. Dejected, and determined never to rely on a man again, Bonnie returned home and took a job as a waitress to make ends meet.

Brown-Eyed Handsome Man

At around the same time, Clyde Chestnut Barrow was getting an apprenticeship in burglary in the company of his brother Marvin Ivan, known to all as 'Buck'. One night the pair broke into a store and stole the safe, loading it on to the back of a truck they had taken earlier that night. Buck's luck ran out when he crashed a stolen car into a lamppost while trying to evade the police. He stubbornly refused to name his partner, who had escaped through a maze of back alleys in the dark, and so was given a stiff sentence, which left Clyde as the family's main breadwinner. Predictably, Clyde returned to burglary and shoplifting, making no effort to hide his face from those who lived to identify him.

Clyde had one asset, though – his looks. He was only 5 ft 7 in (1.70 m) tall, but he was brown-eyed and slim. His large ears, his predominant feature, were made all the more noticeable by his short brown hair. Although he was shy and awkward in the company of strangers, Clyde felt at ease around Bonnie, who saw in him a chance to kick off the dust of the small town and live the sort of life she had only seen in the movies.

Bonnie liked to believe that her backwoods beau had a passion for her and her alone, but Clyde's smouldering emotions were limited to self-loathing and a blind hatred for anyone who got in his way. He hated being a hick, a dirt poor farmer's boy from a small town in Texas, who had to share a room with seven brothers and sisters above a petrol station in West Dallas. His father had found work there after being turned off their farm. Years of poverty had embittered Clyde and left him with no feelings for anyone but himself. It also seems likely that he was confused by his own sexuality. He was in constant turmoil because of his apparent inability to have a normal physical relationship with Bonnie. Bonnie was content just to be with him, but she must have wondered why he did not paw her and pester her to have sex, like the other local boys.

At their first meeting they talked late into the night. Clyde confided that he and his friends were on the run, wanted for hold-ups in the neighbouring counties of Waco and McClennan. If she didn't believe him she could come with them on their next job and see him in action, a dare she readily accepted. Now he had an admirer to dangle on his arm, and a pretty one at that, which would make the other gang members jealous. It is said that Bonnie offered to drive the getaway car, but before the Barrow gang got a chance to make a name for itself Clyde was arrested and held for trial at the Waco County Courthouse. It was a formidable fortress that no ordinary petty hoodlum could have escaped from, but the authorities had not reckoned with the determination of 19-year-old Bonnie Parker. She stole a gun and smuggled it in to Clyde during visiting hours. The evening after the trial Clyde and his cellmate Frank Turner broke out by disarming the guard at gunpoint and locking him in the cell.

One for the family album: Bonnie and Clyde helped inflate their own myth with pictures such as this.

On the Run

The pair evaded local police patrols and headed off for Illinois, where they enjoyed a brief spell robbing fruit stands, petrol stations and train depots. But they were soon back in custody after a witness noted the number plate of their stolen car and reported it to the police. That was a valuable lesson Clyde determined never to forget. When he began his criminal career in earnest with Bonnie they were sure to change number plates immediately after each job.

Back in Waco, Clyde was immediately hauled before a judge who meted out a stiff 14-year sentence with hard labour, to be served at the notorious Eastham Prison Farm, just north of Huntsville. Good-looking young 'punks' (the inmates' term for a male sexual partner) endured continual harassment by older prisoners, as well as routine beatings by sadistic guards. In his desperation to get out of Eastham at any cost, Clyde persuaded another prisoner to fake an accident which cost him two toes. On 8 February 1932 he was discharged due to injury, which allowed him to hobble on crutches to freedom and into the waiting arms of Bonnie.

Prison had not cowed Clyde Barrow. If anything, the experience had fuelled his intense hatred of the law – so much so that he now sought revenge, regardless of the risk to himself. Teaming up with former inmates Ralph Fults and Ray Hamilton he planned a series of stick-ups in small towns across the state, beginning with a hardware store in Kaufman, which just happened to be right across the street from the courthouse. Clyde's arrogance was short-lived, however, because a nightwatchmen set off the alarm. The gang made their getaway by the skin of their teeth, dumping Bonnie by the roadside to save her from capture. But she did not appreciate the gesture – she wanted to ride alongside Clyde and if necessary shoot it out and share the loot. She got her chance shortly after the Kaufman heist when Fults and Hamilton were arrested in separate incidents, the latter after accidentally shooting dead a store owner. This nailed Clyde as an accomplice to murder and made it only a matter of time before the law caught up with him.

A Tight Spot

'I'm just going on 'til they get me. Then I'm out like Lottie's eye.'
CLYDE BARROW, IN A LETTER TO HIS SISTER

In the summer of 1932, just before Hamilton's arrest, a luckless hoodlum almost cost Bonnie and Clyde their liberty. Clyde, Bonnie, Hamilton and one of Hamilton's buddies, Everett Milligan, were driving through Oklahoma when they spotted an open air dance, so they decided to stretch their legs and have a little fun. But no sooner had they stepped unsteadily on to the dance floor, clearly under the influence of illegal hooch, than a couple of local cops approached them and demanded to know why they were drunk in public.

Clyde and Hamilton instinctively went for their weapons, firing at almost point-blank range. They wounded one officer in the gut and killed the other on the spot with a bullet in the throat. In the confusion, Milligan fled. He was captured by a group of irate locals who held him until the police arrived to arrest him. When Milligan identified the shooters as 'The Barrow Gang', an all-state alert was immediately issued. The orders were to bring them in dead or alive.

But Bonnie and Clyde were already heading for the state line, with Hamilton in the back seat. Bonnie suggested that they should hole up at her aunt Nettie's place in Carlsbad, New Mexico, which was so far from the site of the shooting that no lawman would think of looking for them there. Unfortunately for the lovers, Clyde was in a hurry. He raced through the town at top speed, arousing the suspicions of local patrolman Joe Johns, who noted the out-of-state plates.

Johns radioed in with the licence number and when he was told it was a stolen car he followed it to the home of Nettie Stamps. Nettie watched from an upstairs window as the officer approached the front door and she looked on helplessly as Clyde disarmed the officer and walked him to their waiting car.

Patrolman Johns was missing, presumed murdered, for several days and then to everyone's relief he turned up very much alive and unharmed. He was able to tell the newspapers a wild story about how he was kidnapped and forced to pose for photographs with Bonnie and Clyde.

Gun Crazy

Clyde's hair-trigger temper was now almost a natural reflex. He would react like a cornered animal, shooting anyone who looked at him sideways or made a smart remark. In Sherman, Texas, a store owner, Howard Hill, made a sarcastic comment while handing over the day's takings and was shot dead. Clyde was clearly a sociopath, but he was shrewd and cautious when it came to saving his own skin. He deliberately targeted border towns so that Bonnie and he could escape across state lines when the law got too close for comfort. The pair also steered clear of motels, preferring to sleep out in the open during summer and in vacated log cabins whenever they could find one.

But the legend of Bonnie and Clyde belies the fact that they were failures at their chosen profession. By the winter of 1932 it had finally dawned on the couple that robbing tills would never net them the wealth they wanted. The obvious next step was to hold up a bank. Bonnie offered to case the first place they chose, the Oswego Bank in Carthage, Missouri, and she did a fine job of memorizing the layout. But when the day came Clyde pulled out his .38 in full view of a guard, who let fly before he could return fire. With bullets whizzing past his head, Clyde scurried out with nothing more than the handful of dollar bills he had been able to snatch from the teller.

The second job was even more embarrassing. Dismissing the preliminary look around as a waste of time, Clyde rushed in with guns drawn only to find himself in a branch that had closed down some years before. There was not a soul in the place, the tills were covered in cobwebs and the clock had long ceased to tick.

A New Recruit

Homesick at Christmas, the couple returned to Dallas where they snatched fleeting meetings with their families in secret locations. When they left they took with them 16-year-old W.D. Jones, who had pestered Clyde to let him join the gang. Clyde had finally relented, if only to shut the boy up. Though only a teenager, Jones was powerfully built. He could drive a car and handle himself in a fight, which made him quite an asset – or so they hoped. In practice, W.D. proved to be a lethal liability. On Christmas Day the three drove into the town of Temple, cruising the streets in search of a new car to steal. W.D. spotted a brand new Ford V8 Coupe. He boasted that it would enable him to outrace any pursuing patrol car, but when he climbed into the driver's seat he could not start it. Exasperated, Clyde ordered Bonnie to take the wheel of their own car while he pushed Jones aside and attempted to get the now flooded engine to start. The noise of the stuttering Ford brought the local inhabitants to their front windows and the owner racing out into the street. He grabbed Clyde by the tie and clung on as the Ford Coupe kicked into life. Clyde put his foot to the floor. A moment later, as the car accelerated, there was the sickening sound of a gunshot from within; the owner loosened his hold and slid to the ground.

Things went from bad to worse back in Dallas; in the spring of 1933, when a police officer was fatally wounded as the gang shot their way out of an ambush arranged by the authorities. Following this change in police tactics, the gang broke into a government armoury and tooled up to the nines with submachine guns, automatic rifles and gas grenades. Shortly afterwards, they kidnapped a motorcycle cop who had been pursuing them through Springfield, Illinois, and then forced him to steal a car battery and fit it for them.

But the law would not allow itself to be made a fool of and that year the noose tightened around Bonnie and Clyde.

Break-out

In March 1933 Clyde was reunited with his brother Buck, who had finally been released from Huntsville and was now married to a highly strung young woman named Blanche. The brothers thought it would be fun to rent an apartment together and party while the law chased their own shadows. They chose a secluded furnished apartment above a double garage in family-friendly Freeman Park in Joplin. Freeman Park had promised privacy and anonymity, but the gang had not reckoned with their neighbours' insatiable curiosity. Local residents wasted no time in reporting seeing the men carrying armfuls of weapons into the building and they also observed that the curtains were drawn day and night.

Being cooped up in the flat had made the brothers grow restless and they soon tired of playing cards, listening to the radio and reading the newspapers. Why not rob the local bank?

No one knew them around there and they had the perfect hideout to come back to. What they did not know was that the police had the premises under surveillance following the tip-offs, so when Clyde, Buck and Bonnie returned from their 'outing' in a stolen car the authorities were able to match them to the descriptions of the suspects fleeing the scene.

On the morning of 13 April, the police blocked the garage doors with one of their vehicles and began to surround the building. Then Clyde's face suddenly appeared at the window. Someone had made too much noise and gang members were now alerted. Before the cops could run for cover, a full-scale gun battle was under way. Two officers were felled with the first shots, but incredibly none of the gang was hurt. They returned fire through the shattered windows while bullets whizzed and ricocheted all around them, sending a lethal spray of shrapnel and glass in every direction. Blanche became hysterical and ran around screaming, accompanied by the yelping of a puppy tucked into her apron pocket. There was nothing for it but to attempt a break-out.

Staying around to fight would be suicide, so Clyde ordered them all down into the garage, where they piled into their Ford. All except Blanche, that is, who ran out of the back door and across the lawn before Buck could grab her.

Bonnie kept her head down, hugging Clyde around the waist as he started the car. He drove it clean through the closed garage doors, brushing aside the police car that had blocked the entrance. The cops scattered in every direction, recovering in time to see the getaway car careering down the road. Clyde pulled up at the kerb just long enough for Buck to haul his new bride inside and then off he sped, leaving the dazed lawmen wondering what had hit them. But now at least they knew the identity of the two new members of the gang. Among the debris in the apartment they found Blanche's purse and Buck's parole papers.

A Moment of Light Relief

In Ruston, Louisiana, Clyde ordered W.D. to steal a black Chevrolet that had caught his eye and meet up with the gang later. But again the boy bungled the theft. He took so long to get the car into gear that the owner, H. Darby Dillard, was able to borrow his girlfriend's car and take off in hot pursuit with the girl, Sophie Stone, going along for the ride. At the rendezvous point Dillard leapt out of Sophie's car and confronted W.D., but he was surprised to see the boy grin and pull out a gun. Then Clyde, Buck, Bonnie and Blanche pulled up behind them and bundled Dillard and Sophie into their car at gunpoint.

'We're the Barrow gang,' Bonnie informed them proudly.

The 'hostages' grew pale and silent, but they soon relaxed when their kidnappers offered to buy them hamburgers. They also promised to drop them off safely once Clyde got tired of driving the new Chevvy. The atmosphere lightened and the conversation turned to the things they all had in common. But sometime later someone asked Dillard what he did for a living.

'I'm an undertaker,' he told them.

They ditched him and Sophie at the side of the road, giving them a few dollars to get a ride back to town. It was an unnerving portent of their impending fate.

Accident

As the gang raced down Highway 203 towards Wellington, Clyde failed to see a sign warning that a bridge had collapsed. When he saw the gaping chasm ahead it was too late. He braked hard, sending the car into a skid and throwing everyone out into the road. All escaped unscathed except Bonnie, who suffered a vicious-looking gash to her leg. Help was at hand, though, in the form of a farmer, who carried the injured girl back to his home where his wife tended the wound as best she could. W.D. was put on lookout as Buck and Clyde argued about what to do next, but the boy screwed up again when the farmer went to phone the police from a neighbour's house.

'I thought he was going to feed the animals,' W.D. whimpered when Clyde bawled him out.

The gang took off before the law arrived, with the injured Bonnie moaning in pain in the front seat beside Clyde. Blanche whined about how much trouble they were in and W.D. continually complained that he was hungry. Evading road blocks, the gang eventually pulled in to the Twin Cities Tourist Camp in Arkansas, from where Clyde called a doctor. It was a risky business, but Bonnie was clearly in considerable pain and might lose the leg if something was not done to clean the wound and reduce the risk of infection. The doctor believed the story that she had been injured by an exploding oil stove and after doing what he could he recommended that she be taken to hospital. That was obviously out of the question, but Clyde agreed to hire a nurse to attend to her, whose fees were to be paid out of the proceeds of the next two robberies. W.D. and Buck were dispatched to rob a bank in Alma and then a store in nearby Fayetteville, while Clyde sat at the bedside of his beloved, who continually called for her mother while sinking in and out of consciousness. When W.D. and Buck returned they had the money but they were also the bearers of more bad news. They had killed a United States marshal in the grocery store hold-up and now the heat really was on.

But they had a lucky break when they chose their next getaway car. It was owned by a doctor who, quite by chance, had left his medical bag in the vehicle on the day it was driven away by the Barrow gang.

Platte City Shoot-out

The gang's run of luck ended on 18 July 1933. Bonnie was still unable to walk unaided when they rolled into the Red Crown Tourist Camp just outside Platte City, Missouri, but most of the gang would soon be in far worse shape. In a virtual re-run of the Freeman Park shoot-out, the gang found themselves surrounded by dozens of heavily armed officers, while the garage door was barred by an armoured truck. With Clyde at the wheel of their car the gang burst through the garage door, smashing it to matchwood. Clyde then rammed the truck, giving himself just enough room to squeeze past the vehicle and scatter the cordon of armed men. As they roared away, W.D. raked the driver's door of the armoured car with shotgun pellets, putting the officer out of action so that he could not pursue them. But in the mayhem that would have put a Peckinpah movie to shame, Buck was mortally wounded in the head, Blanche was blinded in one eye and W.D. was hit in the shoulder.

When the gang made a dawn stop in Dexfield Park, so that they could lick their wounds, they were again surrounded, this time by about a hundred men armed with hunting rifles, all eager for a share of the reward money. Clyde was winged and Bonnie received a stinging flesh wound, but the pair of them managed to stagger through the woods and vanish among the outlying corn fields, leaving Buck and Blanche behind. Buck bled to death three days later, with half of his head blown away. Blanche survived and was subsequently sentenced to ten years in prison. W.D. disappeared, but he was later arrested in Houston.

By autumn 1933 even the gang's families had resigned themselves to the inevitable. Both the Barrow and the Parker clans had visited a local funeral parlour to make the necessary arrangements, though Clyde and Bonnie were still on the run.

End of the Road

They did not stop running and robbing until 6 May 1934, when they met up with their folks in a rural backwater outside Dallas to enjoy a final family picnic. Bonnie knew the net was closing in and that it was only a matter of time before they met their end. She tried to console her mother.

'Now, Mama, don't get upset... It's coming. You know it. I know it... Mama, when they kill us, don't ever say anything ugly about Clyde.'

That's when Bonnie handed her mother a poem she had recently written, celebrating their notoriety. When the couple said their goodbyes everyone knew they would not see them again – alive, that is.

Henry Methvin, a car thief, had been sprung out of Eastham Prison Farm by Bonnie and Clyde a few months earlier, along with their old gang member Ray Hamilton. But Methvin was to hasten their end by betraying them. During the break-out a guard had been killed, prompting the authorities to hire bounty hunter Frank Hamer to mete out the wages of sin to the perpetrators. The former Texas ranger already had 80 notches on his gun, as well as a reputation for bringing back the bodies of those he had been hired to track down. When Methvin heard that Hamer was on their trail he became a bundle of nerves. Shortly afterwards, the Barrow gang hid out at the farm owned by Iverson (Iver) Methvin, Henry's father, in Acadia, Louisiana. While they were there Henry begged his father to make a deal with the law so he wouldn't end up on a mortuary slab beside Bonnie and Clyde. Iver Methvin saw a chance to secure a lighter sentence for his boy and also get some reward money, so he wasted no time in contacting the authorities. He cut a deal for his son in exchange for setting up an ambush.

Early on the morning of 23 May 1934 Iver Methvin parked his truck by a ditch on the Sailes Road, knowing that the fugitives would have to pass that way on their way back from their regular forays into town. He was confident that they would recognize his vehicle and pull over to see what the trouble was. As Methvin senior paced nervously beside his vehicle Frank Hamer and his men waited under the moss-covered trees that lined the narrow road. There would be no warning this time. Experience had shown them that Bonnie and Clyde would shoot it out rather than surrender.

At 9.15 am a beige 1934 Ford came hurtling down the dirt road, screeching to a halt as it came upon the abandoned truck. From his hidden vantage point Dallas police officer Ted Hinton recognized the silhouette of Clyde Barrow, who was craning his neck in search of the driver.

'It's him!' Hinton mouthed to Hamer, who immediately yelled, 'Shoot!'

Hinton described the last moments of the outlaws in his co-authored account of the killing, *Ambush*.

'... Bonnie screams, and I fire and everyone fires... a drumbeat of shells knifes through the steel body of the car, and glass is shattering. For a fleeting instant, the car seems to melt and hang in a kind of eerie and animated suspension... Clyde is slumped forward, the back of his head a mat of blood... I scramble over the hood of the car and throw open the door on Bonnie's side. The impression will linger with me from this instant – I see her falling out of the opened door, a beautiful and petite young girl... and I smell a light perfume against the burned-cordite smell of gunpowder...'

Hinton recognized Bonnie at once. She had served him when she had worked as a waitress at Marco's Diner in Dallas back in 1929.

The story of Bonnie and Clyde had come full circle – to a dead end.

And Bonnie's prediction had come to pass.

Bonnie and Clyde revelled in their image as modern-day bandit lovers and they took every opportunity to be photographed on the run from the authorities, embracing or kissing as they proudly showed off their arsenal of weapons or their latest getaway car.

Over two years they had terrorized five states – Texas, Oklahoma, Missouri, Louisiana, and New Mexico – killing anyone who got in their way. They gloried in their weaponry and did not give a second thought to the carnage they left in their wake.

LILA AND WILLIAM YOUNG

If the accusations against Canadian 'baby farmers' Lila Gladys and William Peach Young are true, the couple must surely qualify as two of the most heartless killers in history. And yet, against all the odds and in spite of all the evidence accumulated against them, they evaded arrest and prosecution for their crimes.

The daughter of devoutly religious parents, Lila had lived an uneventful life until she met and married William Young, an Oregon-born medical missionary in the Seventh-day Adventist Church. William had failed to qualify as a doctor, but he seemed undeterred by the fact. On the contrary, he was convinced an unshakeable belief in his 'calling' was all he needed to be able to practise medicine on the unfortunate heathens. He could not have heard the call loud enough, though, because he did not venture further than Nova Scotia, where he and his new bride opened the Ideal Maternity Home and Sanitarium in February 1928 as 'an expectant mothers refuge'. Unwed mothers-to-be and those women seeking discreet births were promised 'no publicity' and somewhere to dispose of their unwanted progeny.

It was an offer that soon brought clients from all over the state. The couple's desperate clients thought the term 'disposal' was a euphemism for the arranging of a discreet adoption, but the Youngs were not humanitarians by nature and they had no intention of spending their fees on the long-term care of the infants in their charge.

Their services and their silence did not, of course, come cheap. Married women were required to pay $75 for two weeks' stay at the Sanitarium, while single mothers were charged as much as $200, plus $12 for sundry items such as nappies and $2 a week for nursing while the adoption was being arranged. But the most lucrative item was the $20 charge for infant funerals, of which there were many – far more in fact than could possibly be attributed to natural causes. The Youngs paid local handyman Glen Shatford 50 cents to dispatch the babies. He placed the infant in a butterbox obtained from the grocery store before burying it in waste ground. Shatford later confessed to burying up to 125 infants in a field owned by Lila's unsuspecting parents. Other children were more fortunate. They were farmed out to neighbours, who kept them alive for as long as they could on the mere $3 a week provided by the callous couple. For this long-term bed and board the Youngs charged the mothers $300. Babies of mixed-race parentage and those with disabilities were allegedly starved to death on a diet of water and molasses, presumably in the belief that they were being spared a fate worse than death.

More cost-cutting measures were adopted by the Youngs. Poor girls were given the chance to work off their debt as domestic servants, which cut the costs of their upkeep and ensured that no outsiders could learn the truth of what was happening at the Sanitarium. Trained medical staff were excluded. Clients were billed for the services of two doctors, but in practice Lila acted as midwife while William knelt at the foot of the bed and prayed for the unfortunate sinner.

The Youngs' deviousness and deceit paid real dividends when it came to the fees they charged prospective parents, who willingly handed over up to $1,000 per child for a no-questions-asked adoption, a fee which had increased to $5,000 by the 1940s. By fleecing their clients at both ends of the baby chain the Youngs were estimated to have netted $3.5 million and by the outbreak of the Second World War they had

The Youngs came from deeply religious backgrounds, but they never let that impinge on their money-making activities.

moved into a 54-room mansion. This large building could house up to 70 infants in its nursery and there were private rooms for wealthier clients who were willing to pay a premium for privacy. And there were always additional 'windfalls' to be had from guilt-ridden young mothers who desperately wanted their babies back after they had changed their minds. The price of retrieval was said to be $10,000.

Things Fall Apart

By all accounts the bullish Lila saw her charges as a burden and she was brutal in her handling of the women who came under her care. In March 1936 the couple were charged with the manslaughter of a mother and her baby, but after a three-day trial both were acquitted for lack of evidence. It was not until nine years later that public health officials received so many complaints of insanitary conditions and neglect that they could no longer afford to ignore them. The Youngs' application for a licence to operate under the Maternity Boarding House Act of 1940 was turned down while the complaints against them were being investigated and in spring 1945 the United States Department of Immigration threatened to prosecute the couple for smuggling children across the Canadian border into the United States. Additional charges were brought for practising medicine without a licence, for which they were subsequently convicted, but Lila and William walked free after paying a token fine of $150. Another conviction for selling babies across the United States border followed in June, but again a modest fine of less than $500 was imposed and the Youngs returned to their lucrative baby-farming business.

Greed and Arrogance

Lila's greed and arrogance were ultimately her undoing. She countered the claims made by a local newspaper with a suit for harassment, but the press were not to be bullied or intimidated as easily as her staff. The newspaper persuaded a number of witnesses to come forward with damning testimony at the hearing, which ensured that the claim for damages was summarily dismissed. Furthermore, the maternity home went out of business before the end of the year. After the Youngs had been exposed they were soon filing for bankruptcy to stave off the deluge of claims that followed. They were also forced to sell their property and move to Quebec.

In 1962 alcoholism and cancer claimed the life of William Young and Lila succumbed to leukaemia five years later. She was buried in a plot close to the unmarked graves of her tiny victims.

MARTHA BECK AND RAYMOND FERNANDEZ

Their story could have been ripped from between the covers of the lurid pulp magazines of the period, but every detail revealed in a humid, crowded courtroom in the Bronx during the summer of 1949 was absolutely true. Raymond Martinez Fernandez and his corpulent lover Martha Beck had lured 17 sex-starved single women to their lair and murdered them for their money. Ironically, for a couple who preyed on 'lonely hearts' they were notoriously cold, calculating and emotionless. After one particularly brutal slaying, when Martha murdered a victim's two-year-old daughter by drowning her in a bath, the pair of them went to the cinema, where they consumed a bucket of popcorn and a gallon of lemonade.

They were an odd couple for sure. Thirty-four-year-old Raymond was Hawaii-born, swarthy, slim and a smart dresser, but balding. He was an old-time Lothario who appealed to lonely middle-aged women, but he would have been laughed at if he had tried his obsequious charms on a pretty young girl. He nevertheless boasted that women found him irresistible and that his sexual prowess and charisma were the manifestation of his voodoo powers. His corpulent lover, 29-year-old Martha Beck (born Martha Seabrook), was certainly under his spell. During the long hours of interrogation after their arrest on 28 February

1949, she sat in silent admiration of her lover and freely admitted that she was his sex slave.

Martha's Early Life

Her psychosis was due, it was said, to a glandular abnormality that had accelerated her development, so that she became a sexually active woman while she was still a child. But the condition had also affected her physical development, making her obese. Her adolescence was abnormal, to say the least, because her mother continually chased away teenage boys with verbal abuse and threats of violence, then beat her daughter for encouraging them. Martha became reclusive, a condition which was exacerbated by her failure to find employment as a nurse, despite qualifying first in her class. She was forced to take a job in a funeral parlour where she worked nights, preparing female bodies for burial.

Desperately unhappy, she moved to California in 1942 where she spent her evenings cruising the bars in order to pick up servicemen for sex. When she discovered that she was pregnant she confronted the father, who threatened to kill himself rather than marry her. To save face, she concocted a story about how she had married a naval officer who had been sent overseas. She proudly showed off the ring to her neighbours, but she had in fact bought it herself. After the baby arrived and there was still no sign of the fictitious father, Martha sent herself a fake telegram notifying her of his 'death' on duty. She then received the sympathy she had craved for so long. Shortly afterwards she met a bus driver, Alfred Beck, who made her pregnant, married her out of sympathy and then left her six months later. Now with two young children to look after – Anthony and Carmen – she withdrew into a fantasy world nourished by trashy romantic magazines and dime novelettes. A new job as a nurse at a children's hospital might have been the saving of her, because she worked well and was promoted to superintendent, but her craving for love and sexual satisfaction would not be appeased through daydreams.

A Changed Man

Raymond was a pleasant, amiable young man and a dutiful husband and father until a freak accident altered his personality. While serving aboard a freighter just after the war he was struck on the head by a steel hatch cover, which dented his skull, causing irreparable brain damage. When he was eventually discharged from hospital in March 1946, his gentle, affable personality had been replaced by a quick-tempered, irascible brooding nature and a compulsion to steal items of little value. The habit earned him a one-year prison sentence during which he shared a cell with a practitioner of voodoo, which gave him an obsession with the occult. On his release he went to live with his sister in Brooklyn, but he kept himself to himself. He complained of headaches and rarely left his room except to post letters to solitary women who had advertised in the lonely hearts columns of the national newspapers. When he met them, he seduced them and robbed them of their valuables, trusting that his victims would be too embarrassed to report the thefts to the police. They were humiliated but unharmed – that is, until Raymond claimed his first murder victim in November 1947.

She was divorcee Jane Thompson. He persuaded her to accompany him on a cruise to Spain, ostensibly to visit his wife and child, whom he had not seen since his accident. Mrs Thompson paid for their passage. When they arrived in Spain Raymond introduced Jane Thompson to his wife and at first the two women were on friendly terms. Then on the night of 7 November 1947 a violent disagreement took place between them after which Raymond was seen to leave Mrs Thompson's room in a hurry. The next morning Jane Thompson was found dead, apparently of natural causes. With no reason to suspect foul play, the Spanish authorities waived the need for an autopsy and she was buried with undue haste. Raymond then left his Spanish wife for the second time and returned to the United States, so that he could claim Mrs Thompson's New York apartment and belongings with the aid of a forged will. His criminal career had now begun in earnest.

Love Letters

On Christmas Day 1947 Martha received her one and only reply to an advertisement she had placed in the lonely hearts column of a national magazine. It was from a 'courteous and successful Spanish businessman' who had settled in New York and was now living in a bachelor apartment that was far too large for him alone. However, he hoped one day to share it with a wife. He piled on the sincerity with a trowel, adding that he had deduced from Martha's description that she had 'a full heart and a great capacity for comfort and love'. She responded by sending a group photograph of the hospital staff in which her squat 14-stone frame was discreetly hidden behind a row of colleagues. After a rapid exchange of letters Raymond requested a lock of hair. The love-struck Martha sent it willingly, assuming that it would be treasured as a love token. In fact, Raymond used it for a voodoo ritual, believing that it would bind Martha to him until he could rob her of whatever wealth he imagined she might possess.

But Martha was not to be fleeced and fooled so easily. When Raymond travelled down to Florida on 28 December it was lust at first sight, for her at least. If he was shocked by her appearance and the presence of two children whose existence she had not even hinted at, then he did not let on. He indulged her in fantasies of wedded bliss, but as soon as he was back in New York he wrote to tell her that any thoughts of marriage must have been a misunderstanding on her part. Martha was not to be shaken off so lightly. Packing a suitcase, she caught the next train to New York with her two kids in tow. When the unlikely looking Romeo answered the door on 18 January he found a new family camped on the front step. Evidently his voodoo charms must have been more potent than he had thought. He took them in against his better instincts and Martha went straight into her devoted slave routine. This convinced Raymond that he was on to a good thing if he could string her along without any further talk of marriage.

But the kids would have to go. Incredibly, Martha relented and one morning she dropped her two offspring at the local Salvation Army shelter without so much as a note of explanation. It was as if they were two sacks of charity cast-offs. She did not see them again until she was in prison.

In Fernandez' (right) thrall or a willing accomplice? Martha Beck (left) preyed on women who were very similar to herself.

Strange Double Act

Having proved Martha's unquestioning obedience, Raymond took her into his confidence. He explained the scam he was operating and together they found her a role to play in the scheme, one that would make his story more convincing. They scoured the country in the following months, systematically working through a list of would-be wives. Posing as either his sister or his sister-in-law, Martha played the role of chaperone. At one point she even slept in the marriage bed with the new bride, to prevent the couple from consummating their union. At this stage their crime was heinous but not homicidal. They fleeced the gullible and lived off the proceeds, but it rarely amounted to more than a few thousand dollars.

But at the beginning of 1949 Martha's jealousy took a vicious turn and she bludgeoned her lover's new bride to death with a hammer after strangling her with a scarf. Janet Fay was a devout Catholic whom Raymond had ensnared by appealing to her religious faith. He played the upright, moral Christian husband all the way to the altar, but when Martha walked in on them lying naked in bed on their wedding night Raymond demanded that Martha silence her in any way she could. It is not known if he struck Janet with the hammer and Martha strangled her or if it was the other way round. Maybe Martha committed the crime alone, but that seems unlikely. In her confession she claimed to have no recollection of the killing. Whatever the truth, they both colluded in the cover-up. They wrapped the bloody corpse in towels and bed sheets and stored it in a closet and then they both went to sleep as if nothing had happened.

The next day they purchased a large trunk. After cramming the body into it they took it to the home of Raymond's sister, who unwittingly allowed them to store it in her basement.

There it remained until 15 January, when Raymond returned to collect it. He buried it that night in the basement of a rented house. After

Janet's murder the couple cashed her cheques and created the illusion that she was still alive and well by sending cheery letters to her relatives. But these messages only aroused her family's curiosity, because they were all typed. Janet Fay had never learned to use a typewriter.

The Widow and Her Daughter

Meanwhile, the killer couple had moved on to Grand Rapids, Michigan where Raymond seduced their next victim. Her name was Delphine Downing and she was a 41-year-old widow and mother with whom he had been corresponding under the pen name 'Charles Martin'. Raymond was a quick worker and within weeks courtship had moved on to sex. But one morning Delphine went into the bathroom and caught a glimpse of the real Raymond Fernandez without his toupee. She went into hysterics and accused him of deceit. The screaming roused Martha who persuaded the distraught woman to take a sleeping pill and go back to bed. During all of this commotion Delphine's two-year-old daughter, Rainelle, started to cry, at which point Martha lost control. She throttled the child until she lost consciousness.

Raymond panicked at the thought of Delphine waking up and seeing the girl's bruises, so he went to fetch a gun that had belonged to her husband. When he returned to the bedroom he wrapped a blanket around it to deaden the sound and then he fired one shot at point-blank range. Delphine was dead. They buried her in the basement and covered the hole with cement. Then for two days they ransacked the place where she lived, taking everything of value. By that time the little girl had regained consciousness and was crying for her mother. Unable to cope, Martha drowned the toddler in a tub, after which she too was buried in the basement. Then they went to the cinema, but on their return they found two police officers waiting for them. The neighbours had reported hearing a child crying for the past two days and there had been no sign of its mother.

At the Kent County district attorney's office the couple signed a 73-page confession detailing their crimes, in return for an assurance that they would not stand trial in New York, which had the death penalty. Michigan did not. There was an understanding that Raymond would probably be released in six years, although with three murders hanging over him it is almost impossible to believe that he would ever have been allowed to walk free. The press showed the couple no mercy, describing them as degenerates and demanding the death penalty. Nor was there a shred of sympathy from the district attorney's office. The Kent County authorities finally bowed to public pressure and on 8 March 1949 Beck and Fernandez were handed over to the New York prosecutors for trial in relation to the murder of Janet Fay. The shadow of the electric chair loomed ever larger.

The Hottest Ticket in Town

Despite the blistering heat the courtroom was packed when the trial opened on 9 June 1949. The *New York Times* reported that many female spectators gladly skipped their lunch to keep their seats. When the couple's confession was read out aloud during the proceedings it included stories of three-way strip poker, with Raymond as the prize.

On the day that Martha finally took the stand, two dozen extra policemen were called in to hold back the crowds jostling for a place. She described the sordid sex acts she and Raymond had indulged in as part of his voodoo rituals, but she refused to find such activities abnormal.

'We loved each other and I consider it absolutely sacred... You referred to the lovemaking as abnormal but for the love I had for Fernandez, nothing is abnormal!... a request from Mr Fernandez to me is a command. I loved him enough to do anything he asked me to!'

She also said, 'Raymond got quite a kick out of the photographs some of the old hags sent him, expecting to correspond with him.'

But she claimed to have no recollection of the murder of Janet Fay, only of the lifeless body lying at her feet. It was her idea, she said, to wrap a scarf around Mrs Fay's neck, but it had been in an effort to save her, not strangle her. Her training as a nurse had taught her that 'a tourniquet about the neck would stop bleeding from the head'. Her self-deception was staggering.

On 18 August 1949 the jury returned after an all-night sitting. Their verdict was delivered to an empty courtroom. It was 8.30 am and the spectators had not expected such a quick decision. The judge noted the verdict – both defendants were found guilty in the first degree – and he postponed sentencing until 22 August.

On that day Raymond Fernandez and Martha Beck were both sentenced to die in the electric chair at Sing Sing. While they lingered on Death Row Raymond wrote letters of love and longing to his first wife, giving little thought to Martha who agonized over her faithless lover, insulting him one moment and forgiving him the next.

'What do they expect me to do? Sit here and let him destroy the one thread of decency I have left? He has done so much talking about how he has me wrapped around his little finger that it was a blow to his ego when I unwrapped myself and forgot about him... All I can say is: what a character! Oh yes, he's brave when it comes to talk and hurting others – he can kill without batting an eyelash – but to hurt himself – he'd never do it. It takes a man to kill himself. Not a snivelling, low-down, double-crossing, lying rat like him!'

But on the last day of their lives, 8 March 1951, they made up, sending notes between the cell blocks professing eternal affection for each other.

'The news brought to me that Martha loves me is the best I've had in years,' said Raymond. 'Now I'm ready to die! So tonight I'll die like a man!'

But he died a pitiful figure, having to be carried to the death chamber because he was too frightened to walk unaided. His last words were delivered in a voice that was broken with emotion.

'I want to shout it out. I love Martha! What do the public know about love?'

Martha's final statement was equally hysterical.

'What does it matter who is to blame? My story is a love story, but only those tortured with love can understand what I mean. I was pictured as a fat, unfeeling woman... I am not unfeeling, stupid or moronic... in the history of the world how many crimes have been attributed to love?'

She had difficulty squeezing into the chair as the matrons strapped her down. Then she mouthed her last words.

'So long.'

At 11.24 pm the current surged through her. Minutes later she was officially pronounced dead.

WERNER BOOST AND FRANZ LORBACH

In the chaos of post-war Germany many murders went undetected and unsolved. It was open season for serial killers, who could settle old scores or simply hunt for 'sport', secure in the knowledge that their killings would be attributed to the Russian invaders or desperate German deserters. No one had the resources, the energy or the inclination to investigate civilian deaths. Germany was a country overrun with refugees, liberated prisoners and 'displaced persons', all without identification documents. At Helmstedt, in Lower Saxony, several refugees had been shot as they attempted to escape from the Russian zone, but not by the sentries who patrolled the new border. They were the first victims of former German conscript Werner Boost, who had acquired a taste for killing in the final year of the war and now found that he could satisfy his bloodlust by targeting fleeing refugees as they raced across the open fields to freedom in the West. It was like shooting rabbits, only the thrill was more intense. And it was addictive.

The war did not make Werner a murderer – he had displayed a mean streak even in childhood, for by the age of six he had been convicted of theft and sent to a home for delinquent boys in Magdeburg. However, when the Russians reinforced their patrols along the border at Helmstedt he abandoned his hunting to concentrate on stealing scrap metal from graveyards. After all, there was no money to be made from shooting refugees who had nothing but the clothes on their back.

But in 1951 he was caught and sent to prison. On his release he met a simple-minded and gullible soul named Franz Lorbach, who believed Werner's heroic war stories and became his trusting sidekick. Like the somnambulistic Cesare in the German impressionist film *The Cabinet of Dr. Caligari*, Lorbach submitted to the will of his domineering partner by aiding him in the robbery and murder of courting couples, who always chose remote locations and did not put up any resistance. Werner held them at gunpoint while Franz drugged them with a concoction his master had created. Then with their victims sedated Werner would shoot the man and rape the woman, before killing her too. If they found money or other valuables on their victims, that would be a bonus.

But they had not planned for the unexpected. One night in 1956 they came across two male lovers. Dr Serve from Düsseldorf and his male friend were sharing an intimate moment when they were accosted by Werner and Franz. Werner did not wait to administer the drug but shot the doctor without thinking and then ordered Franz to kill the man's companion. But Franz bungled it, which enabled the young man to give detectives a detailed description of his attackers.

However, the killings continued. The next couple were murdered with a bullet to the head and cyanide before being partially burned near the scene and two further victims were drowned in a lake in their own car after being knocked unconscious. But it was the last thrill that Werner would enjoy at someone else's expense. On 6 June 1956 a labourer saw him spying on a courting couple. The man tackled him and alerted the lovers, who sent for the police. When Franz read about Werner's arrest in the morning paper he walked into the local police station and made a full and detailed confession. His 'master' was sentenced to life imprisonment.

CHARLES STARKWEATHER AND CARIL FUGATE

The case of Charles Starkweather and Caril Fugate is a fascinating if shocking one. Charles Starkweather, a rebellious 19-year-old, modelled himself on James Dean. Caril Fugate was his underage girlfriend. Together, they went on an unprecedented killing spree, murdering family members, friends, strangers and anyone else who got in their way. Eventually, the law caught up with them and they were found guilty of a string of murders. Starkweather was sentenced to death; being only 14 at the time of her conviction, Caril Fugate's sentence was commuted to life imprisonment. Just why the pair suddenly showed such unbelievable brutality to a series of innocent victims, leaving a trail of bloodshed behind them wherever they went, remains to this day something of a mystery.

Charles Starkweather hailed from Nebraska, and was one of seven children. His family was poor but seemingly settled. However, when he went to school he was teased and became oversensitive, often getting into fights with other boys in his class. The frenzied nature of his attacks was remarkable, and by the time he was a teenager, he had developed a reputation for violence. He and his close friend Bob Von Busch idolized the film star James Dean, imitating their hero down to the last detail, a pose that impressed Barbara Fugate, Bob's girlfriend, and her younger sister Caril.

Charles was not a very intelligent young man, but this did not bother the young, impressionable Caril, who was herself none too bright. The pair started going out together, despite the fact that Caril was only 13. Soon it became clear that Charles was besotted with his new girlfriend, boasting that he was going to marry her and that she was pregnant with his child – a claim that, even though untrue, did not endear him greatly to Caril's parents.

Fatal Robbery

Starkweather left school aged 16 and began work at a newspaper warehouse. However, he soon gave up the job, and took on work as a garbage man, mainly so that he could see more of Caril after she came out of school. He had moved out of his family home into a rooming house, but now found he could not pay the rent. He became increasingly frustrated by his life of poverty, and felt trapped in a situation that seemed to hold no future for him or his girlfriend. Finally, his patience snapped when he was refused credit to buy Caril a stuffed toy animal at a gas station, and he decided to take matters into his own hands.

At 3am on a freezing cold night in December 1957, Starkweather returned to the gas station. There he robbed the attendant who had previously refused him credit, 21-year-old Robert Colville, took him out to a deserted area and shot him.

His next crime was even more unbelievable. He drove to Caril's house and, after a violent altercation, shot her mother Velda Bartlett, her stepfather Marion Bartlett and stabbed her baby half-sister Betty Jean to death. Then he dragged Velda's body to the toilet outside, put Marion's in the chicken coop and stuffed the baby's into a garbage box. When Caril returned home from school, the pair cleaned up the blood and spent several days in the family home doing as they pleased. Visitors

Charles Starkweather shot his girlfriend Caril Fugate's mother while she cleaned up the mess.

to the house were told to go away because everyone 'had the flu'. By the time the police investigated, the couple were on the run. The first victim they killed together was August Meyer, a bachelor of 72 who had been a family friend of the Starkweathers for many years. They shot him, hid his body in an outhouse and made off with his guns. They then hitched a ride with teenagers Robert Jensen and Carol King. They shot Jensen repeatedly in the head, while King was stabbed to death and left naked from the waist down.

Hostage or Accomplice?

The couple's next stop was a wealthy part of town where Starkweather had once collected garbage. They called on Clara Ward and her maid Lillian Fencl. Starkweather ordered Mrs Ward to make breakfast for them before stabbing her to death. When her husband came home, a fight ensued and he was killed. Finally, the maid was tied to a bed and stabbed to death. The pair then made off in the Wards' black Packard. On their journey, just for good measure, they shot a travelling shoe salesman, Merle Collison.

Finally, after a car chase, police arrested Starkweather and Fugate in Wyoming. To protect herself, Fugate alleged that she had been taken hostage by Starkweather. In response, Starkweather claimed that some of the murders were her doing. No one believed their stories; both were tried for murder and both were found guilty.

Starkweather was sentenced to death and Fugate, because of her age, received a life sentence. Their extraordinary story, which seemed motivated not just by extreme violence but also by a curiously childlike lack of intelligence, inspired several successful Hollywood movies.

KENNETH AND IRENE DUDLEY

If evidence is needed to support the assertion that killing others is a form of insanity, then one need look no further than the case of itinerant carnival workers Kenneth and Irene Adelle Dudley, who allowed six of their children to die of malnutrition and neglect and then drove across the southern states, dumping the bodies along the route.

According to the confession drawn out of Irene Dudley, her husband was a cruel and vindictive man who starved and brutalized his children in an attempt to teach them discipline. He slapped one of his girls for 'moving a lot', and stuck four fingers down another child's throat for 'hollering'.

Irene denied she had taken part in the abuse and claimed she had secretly fed the children whenever she could. However, the fact that she had given birth to so many children while knowing of her husband's cruelty suggested she condoned his behaviour. And the fact that she had made no attempt to leave him and take the children with her, or even complain to the authorities, made her an accessory in the eyes of the law. Her pleas of innocence following her indictment for murder fell on stony ground. The evidence of her willing participation in the deaths – and disposal – of six of her ten children was overwhelming.

Fatal Neglect

The sad and tragic story of the Dudley children unravelled on 9 February 1961, when the first corpse was spotted on Route 1, near Lawrenceville, Virginia. When the young female victim was taken to the local mortuary the medical examiner found evidence of abuse – specifically bruises, broken bones and open sores. The official cause of death, however, was malnutrition and exposure, suggesting that the child had been left to die at the side of the highway in the biting winter winds.

A couple had been questioned at the same spot by a Highway Patrol officer three days earlier, so the local law enforcement authorities immediately responded with a warrant for their detention. The officer had become suspicious when he had seen their battered sedan parked at the roadside and he had been concerned by the poor physical appearance of the children. On the following day the Dudleys were arrested near Fuqua, North Carolina and brought in to Brunswick County jail, where they were questioned at length. At the same time officers traced the couple's two eldest married daughters to addresses in New York. Those interviews revealed that the couple had begun their journey three years earlier in July 1958, with six children in tow. By the time of their arrest, only two-year-old Christine had survived.

Retracing the couple's epic trek across the southern United States in search of work, detectives were able to piece together the terrible events body by body. Four-year-old Claude had been the first to succumb. His body had been wrapped in a blanket and left at Lakeland, Florida on 19 November 1958. Just over a year later, on New Year's Day 1960, the lifeless bodies of ten-year-old Norman and his eight-year-old brother Charles were found floating in Lake Pontchartrain, Louisiana. They had been wrapped in a blanket and tied together before being thrown off a bridge like a sack of garbage. Toddler Deborrah Jane was dispatched in a cardboard box and left on a rubbish heap in Kentucky on 21 May 1960, followed by her nine-year-old sister Carol Ann, who was left by the roadside in freezing temperatures near Lawrenceville on 9 February 1961.

As the details of the family history were unearthed a file on another child was brought to the attention of the detectives. Created in Syracuse, New York in 1946, this record described how Kenneth Dudley had served a term of imprisonment for improper burial. Although no evidence could be produced to support a prosecution for murder, there was overwhelming evidence of cruelty and neglect of such magnitude that it had led directly to the deaths of all six children.

Irene gave a statement to the police. 'Because we had no money at times the children were denied food, as punishment for misbehaviour. At times, my husband and I ate while the children had nothing. We were better off than the children.'

The couple underwent psychiatric evaluation before receiving lengthy jail sentences for treating their children with so much cruelty.

IAN BRADY AND MYRA HINDLEY

ritain has had other prolific serial killers than Ian Brady and Myra Hindley, but none has attracted so much attention or become so clearly the embodiment of evil as this couple, the so-called 'Moors Murderers' who brutally tortured and killed at least five children in the early 1960s. At the heart of the horror was the role of Myra Hindley, as, up to that time, only men were known to carry out serial sex murders of children. That a woman should have joined in seemed so utterly against nature that Hindley became Britain's number one hate figure, reviled even more than the principal agent of their crimes, Ian Brady.

Put Into Care

Ian Brady was born in Glasgow, Scotland, on 2 January 1938. His mother, Peggy Stewart, was unmarried at the time and unable to support her child. She gave her baby, aged four months, over to the care of John and Mary Sloane, a couple with four children of their own. Peggy continued to visit her son for a while, though not revealing that she was actually his mother. The visits stopped when she moved to Manchester, England, with her new husband, Patrick Brady, when her son was 12 years old.

Ian was a difficult child, intelligent but a loner. In his teens, despite having passed the entrance examination to a good school, Shawlands

Academy, he went completely off the rails. He became fascinated by Nazi Germany and by Adolf Hitler in particular, missed school frequently and committed burglaries. By the age of 16, he had been arrested three times. He was only saved from reform school when he agreed to leave Glasgow and go to live with his natural mother Peggy in Manchester.

When he arrived in Manchester, in late 1954, he made an effort to fit in, taking his stepfather's name. He worked as a market porter, but within a year he was in trouble again. He was jailed for theft, and while imprisoned seems to have decided on his future career: professional criminal. With this in mind, he studied book-keeping. On his release, he found work as a labourer while looking for a suitable criminal enterprise. Unable to find anything, he put his new skill to more conventional use and got a job as a book-keeper with a company called Millwards Merchandising. A year later a new secretary arrived to work there: Myra Hindley.

Baby-sitter

Myra Hindley had a slightly more conventional upbringing than Brady. She was born in Manchester on 23 July 1942, the oldest child of Nellie and Bob. During the war years, while Bob was in the army, the family lived with Myra's grandmother, Ellen Maybury. Later, when Bob and Nellie had trouble coping in the post-war years, Myra went back to live with her grandmother, who was devoted to her. Throughout her school years Myra was seen as a bright, though not overambitious, child with a love of swimming. In her teens, she was a popular baby-sitter.

Leaving school at 16, she took a job as a clerk in an engineering firm. Soon afterwards, she got engaged to a local boy, Ronnie Sinclair. However, she broke off the engagement, having apparently decided that she wanted more excitement in life. That wish was all too horribly granted when she took a new job and found herself working with Ian Brady.

Ian Brady was the illegitimate son of a waitress; Hindley was attracted by his sullen manner and introspective nature.

Hindley soon fell for the sullen, brooding Brady. It took him a year to reciprocate her interest, but once they became lovers, he realized he had found the perfect foil for his increasingly dark fantasies. Brady had spent much of the previous few years obsessively reading. Particular favourites were Dostoyevsky's *Crime and Punishment*, Hitler's *Mein Kampf* and the Marquis de Sade's *Justine*, among other, less elevated books on sadomasochism. Brady increasingly saw himself as some kind of superman, beyond the bounds of good and evil. The devoted Myra lapped all this up. During their first years together she transformed herself with hair dye and make-up into the Aryan blonde of Brady's fantasies. She gave up seeing her friends and devoted herself utterly to her lover.

In 1964, Brady introduced Hindley to the next stage in their relationship: a life of crime. His first notion was a bank robbery. The dutiful Myra joined a gun club and obtained two weapons for him. However, before the robbery could be carried out, Brady changed his mind. It was not robbery he wanted to commit but murder.

The couple's first victim was 16-year-old Pauline Reade. The couple waylaid the teenager on the way to a dance on 12 July 1963. They lured her on to Saddleworth Moor, where Brady raped her and cut her throat. They then buried her there.

Having got away with the crime, on 11 November Brady decided it was time to kill again. The victim this time was a 12-year-old boy, John Kilbride, whom they abducted from Ashton-under-Lyne. Seven months later, in June 1964, another 12-year-old, Keith Bennett, was abducted from near his home in Manchester. Both boys were raped, murdered and buried on the moors.

After six more months they struck again, on Boxing Day, 26 December 1964. This time they took a girl: ten-year-old Lesley Ann Downey. With Hindley's assistance, Brady took pornographic photographs of Downey, which he planned to sell to rich perverts. The couple, now entirely engrossed in their evil, even made an audio tape of their torture of the terrified little girl. Finally, Brady raped her and either he or Hindley – depending on whose account you believe – strangled her, before they buried her on the moors with the others.

Myra Hindley in the clothes she wore to befriend and ultimately kidnap the children she and Brady murdered.

Brady took to boasting about his exploits to Hindley's brother-in-law, David Smith. Angered when Smith did not believe him, Brady made Hindley bring Smith to their house on 6 October 1965, just as he was about to dispatch his latest victim, 17-year-old Edward Evans. Smith was not impressed but horrified and went to the police the next morning. They raided the house and found Evans' body there. Further investigation soon led them to start digging on the moors, where they discovered the bodies of Downey and Kilbride. Next, they found a box containing the photos and the tape documenting Downey's murder. At trial both Brady and Hindley tried to pin the blame on David Smith, but the sensational evidence of the tape led to them both being convicted of murder.

Brady and Hindley each received a life sentence. Brady later confessed to five other murders, which remain unproven. In 2002, he wrote a book on serial killers that caused controversy in Britain. That same year, Myra Hindley died in prison. In May 2017, Brady died at Ashworth Hospital on Merseyside, taking the secret of the burial place of his final victim, Keith Bennett, to the grave.

MYRON LANCE AND WALTER KELBACH

I t is a depressing but undeniable fact that some criminals are beyond rehabilitation. Even after their conviction they exhibit no signs of remorse and may even revel in their notoriety and the power of life and death they held over their victims. Sadistic sex killers Walter Kelbach, 28, and Myron Lance, 25, are just two examples of offenders whose release even the most liberal prison reformer would not support.

Both men were ex-convicts and drug addicts. They were also predatory homosexuals with a strong sadistic streak. In December 1966, when their law-abiding neighbours in Salt Lake City were preparing to celebrate Christmas, Kelbach and Lance were high on something other than the festive spirit. They swallowed a potent cocktail of pills and alcohol and then drove to a petrol station, where they robbed the 18-year-old attendant, Stephen Shea, of $147. Then they forced him into their car and drove to a deserted spot, where they raped and killed him. After the pair had argued over who would have the pleasure of murdering the boy they finally decided to settle the matter by tossing a coin. Kelbach, the 'winner', stabbed Shea five times in the chest with a stiletto.

The following day Lance demanded a rematch, so the pair drove to another filling station, where they abducted the attendant Michael Holtz. Again the victim was sodomized by both men before being left to writhe in agony on the ground while they flipped a coin to decide who would kill him. Lance went on to stab Holtz through the heart.

On 21 December Lance and Kelbach targeted taxi driver Grant Strong. Sensing there was something untoward about his two passengers, Strong pulled over to report his suspicions to his supervisor. It was agreed that he would flip the switch of his radio transmitter if he was in trouble, which he did just moments after driving on.

Kelbach then put a gun to the driver's head and demanded money, but after he had grabbed the night's takings he shot Strong anyway. 'Blood flew everywhere,' Kelbach grinned, recalling the scene. 'Oh boy! I never seen so much blood!' The police arrived too late to save the taxi driver and they had no idea of the whereabouts of his assailants.

While the authorities converged on the scene of their latest crime Lance and Kelbach were strolling into Lolly's Tavern, near Salt Lake City airport. Before anyone had a chance to ask them what they were drinking Lance shot customer James Sizemore and then ordered the bartender to empty the till. Then both men shot him, before blasting wildly at the customers, two of whom died. But the barman managed to retrieve a weapon from under the counter. He fired at the gunmen as they walked away, but failed to hit either of them.

The duo were captured a couple of hours later and were subsequently convicted on five counts of first degree murder. The mandatory sentence in the state of Utah was death, but an appeal to the United States Supreme Court resulted in the sentences being commuted to life imprisonment because the death penalty was ruled unconstitutional.

The pair remain in prison and are stubbornly unrepentant. 'I haven't any feelings toward the victims,' Walter Kelbach told a reporter from NBC in 1972. 'I don't mind people getting hurt because I just like to watch it.'

FRED AND ROSEMARY WEST

The crimes of Fred and Rosemary West utterly shocked the people of Britain when they emerged in 1994. It was not simply that nine bodies were found buried under the couple's house in Gloucester. It was not that one of the bodies belonged to their own daughter, Heather. It was not even the discovery of other bodies belonging to Fred West's first wife and child. What was almost unbearable for people to accept was that this bloody carnage had taken place in an apparently normal family home, a place full of children and visitors, presided over by a happily married couple.

Virtually Illiterate

To understand the crimes of the Wests one has, as so often in such cases, to go back to their early childhoods. Fred West was one of six children born to Walter and Daisy West in 1941, in Much Marcle on the edge of the Forest of Dean. At the time, the village was a very poor rural backwater. Fred was very close to his mother. He claimed that his father sexually abused his sisters, though whether this was actually the case is not known. He did badly at school and was virtually illiterate when he left, aged 15. He worked, like his father and grandfather before him, as a farmhand. At the age of 17 he had a serious motorbike accident in which he sustained a head injury – a common factor in the backgrounds of a large number of serial killers. Two years later, he was arrested for having sex with a 13-year-old girl. He managed to avoid going to prison after his lawyer told the judge that Fred suffered from epileptic fits, but his parents threw him out of the family home for a while.

A Different Story?

In 1962, Fred met Catherine 'Rena' Costello, a young woman with a record of delinquency and prostitution. They fell in love, moved to her native Scotland and got married, despite the fact that she was already pregnant by an Asian bus driver. The child, Charmaine, was born in 1963. The following year they had their own child, Anna Marie. They then moved back to Gloucester, where they split up. Fred took up with a friend of Rena, Anne McFall. By 1967 McFall was pregnant with Fred's child, and demanded that he divorce Rena and marry her. This provoked Fred's first murder: he killed McFall, dismembered her body and that of their unborn baby, and buried them near the trailer park in which they had been living. Curiously, he cut off the tops of McFall's fingers and toes before burying her. This was to become a Fred West trademark.

Following McFall's murder, Rena moved back in with Fred. During this period, he is thought to have murdered 15-year-old Mary Bastholm, whom he abducted from a bus stop in Gloucester. Later the couple split up again, and it was then that Fred met a young girl who turned out to be as vicious and depraved as he was.

Rosemary Letts was born in November 1953 in Devon. Her mother, Daisy Letts, suffered from severe depression. Her father, Bill Letts, was a schizophrenic who had sexually abused her. A pretty, rather slow child, she became fat and sexually precocious as a teenager. When she met Fred West, 12 years her senior, he seemed to be the man of her dreams. Soon afterwards, however, Fred was sent to prison for non-payment of fines. By then Rose, not yet 16, was pregnant with his child.

Missing

When Fred came out of jail, Rose went to live with him, Charmaine and Anna Marie, and in 1970 gave birth to Heather. The following year, while Fred was once again in prison, Charmaine went missing. Rose told people that Charmaine's mother Rena had come to take her back. In fact Rose herself had murdered Charmaine while in the grip of one of the ferocious tempers her other children would become all too familiar with.

When Fred was released from prison, he buried the body of the child under the house. Not long after, Rena did indeed come looking for Charmaine. Fred killed her too, and buried her in the countryside.

In 1972, Fred and Rose married and had a second child, Mae. They moved to a house in Cromwell Street, Gloucester. There, they began to indulge in deviant sex, using the cellar of the house as a perverse sexual playpen. They even raped their own eight-year-old daughter Anna Marie there. Later that year, they employed 17-year-old Caroline Owens as a nanny. Owens rejected their sexual advances – Rose by now was having sex with both men and women – so they raped her. She escaped and told the police, but when the matter came to trial in January 1973 the magistrate, appallingly, believed Fred's word over that of Owens' and let the Wests off with a fine.

At least Owens escaped with her life. Their next nanny, Lynda Gough, ended up dismembered and buried under the cellar. The following year, in which Rose gave birth to another child, Stephen, the couple murdered 15-year-old Carol Ann Cooper. In late December, they abducted university student Lucy Partington, tortured her for a week and then murdered, dismembered and buried her.

The Wests' perversions became ever more extreme. Over the next 18 months they killed three more women: Therese Siegenthaler, Shirley Hubbard and Juanita Mott. Hubbard and Mott had been subjected to almost unimaginable tortures: their bodies, when exhumed, were trussed in elaborate bondage costumes. Hubbard's head had been wrapped entirely with tape, with only a plastic tube inserted in her nose to allow her to breathe.

In 1977, Rose, who was also by now working as a prostitute, became pregnant by one of her clients. However, at around the same time, their latest lodger Shirley Robinson, an 18-year-old ex-prostitute, became pregnant with Fred's child. Rose was angry about this development, and decided the girl had to go. In December 1977, she was murdered and, as the cellar was now full, the Wests buried her in the back garden, along with her unborn baby.

In May 1979 the Wests killed once again. The victim this time was teenager Alison Chambers – another body for the back garden. Then, as far as is known, the Wests stopped killing for pleasure. It may be that they carried on killing and that their victims were never found; it may be that they found other sources of sexual excitement. Exactly what happened is still not known.

During the 1980s, Rose had three more children – two by another client, one more with Fred. She continued to work as a prostitute, specializing in ever more extreme bondage. Fred found a new interest in making videotapes of Rose having sex, and continued to abuse his daughters, until Heather told a friend about her home life. Her friend's parents told the Wests about Heather's allegation and Fred responded by killing her, the last of his known victims.

Under the Patio

It was not until 1992 that a young girl whom the Wests had raped went to the police. On 6 August that year, police arrived at Cromwell Street with a search warrant to look for pornography and evidence of child abuse: they found plenty, and so arrested Rose for assisting in the rape of a minor. Fred was arrested for rape and sodomy of a minor. Anna Marie made a statement supporting the allegation, as did their oldest son Stephen, but following threats from the Wests they withdrew them

Fred and Rose West made a terrifying couple. Violence, rape, incest, torture, voyeurism and paedophilia were all part of a normal day for the Wests.

and the case collapsed. Meanwhile, the younger children had been taken into care. While there, care assistants heard the children joke about their older sister Heather being buried under the patio. A day's digging revealed human bones – and not just Heather's. Eventually, a total of nine bodies were found in the garden. Other bodies buried elsewhere were later exhumed.

On 13 December 1994, Fred and Rosemary West were charged with murder. A week later, Fred hanged himself in prison with strips of bed sheet. Rose's defence tried to put the blame for the murders on Fred, but she was duly sentenced to life imprisonment.

DAVID AND CATHERINE BIRNIE

They were dubbed the 'Moorhouse Murderers' after their home address 3 Moorhouse Street, Willagee, Australia. Serial killers, together they had strangled and bludgeoned. Four young women and one girl had died at their hands. David and Catherine Birnie were seen as monsters, were hated and threatened. Yet David was small and slight, not much bigger than his wife Catherine. At first glance, this ordinary-looking couple seemed incapable of harming anyone. But that initial impression was all that was needed to lure their victims into their trap.

David Birnie was born in Subiaco, a suburb of Perth, on 16 February 1951, which is where he spent his childhood. The Birnies were seen as a problem family by their neighbours and fellow parishioners at Wattle Grove Baptist Church. There was gossip about affairs, drinking and incest, and the authorities took the Birnie children away from their parents on more than one occasion.

David met Catherine, who was just three months his junior, when her family moved in next door. The two soon became a couple. Catherine was an unhappy girl with no real friends. She had never known her mother, who had died when she was an infant, and she rarely saw her father. Although she had been raised by her grandparents, she felt unwanted, so David provided the affection that had been lacking in her life.

Attempted Rape

Never a good student, David left school at the age of 15, intending to become a jockey. He became an apprentice at a nearby race track, where he worked for trainer Eric Parnham. There are conflicting accounts of David's behaviour during this time. Parnham maintains that David was a good worker who never did anything wrong, while others claim that he often displayed cruelty towards the horses. Whatever the truth, there was no doubt about the fact that he attempted to rob and rape the elderly landlady of his boarding house. The assault brought his job with Parnham to an end, together with all of his dreams of becoming a jockey.

Fortunately for David his landlady did not report his crime to the police and yet he learned nothing from the experience. He began burgling people's homes, often accompanied by Catherine. On 11 June 1969 the pair appeared at the Perth Police Court, where they pleaded guilty to 11 charges of breaking, entering and stealing. Among the stolen goods were items of welding equipment, which they used in an attempt to break into the safe of a drive-in cinema.

David was jailed for nine months – his first prison sentence – while Catherine was placed on probation. The authorities dealt leniently with Catherine because of her condition. The 18-year-old girl was pregnant with another man's child. Three weeks later, the couple were brought before the Supreme Court, where they faced more charges of breaking, entering and stealing. After pleading guilty, David's sentence was increased by a further three years, while Catherine's probation was extended by a further four years.

After serving just one year in prison David managed to escape. During his brief period of freedom he committed 53 further offences. Most of them involved breaking, entering and stealing, but mixed in with his haul were 100 sticks of gelignite and 120 detonators. As before, Catherine had been a willing accomplice. There was nothing she would not do for David, she told the court.

This time the authorities were not so forgiving. Catherine received a six-month jail sentence and her baby was taken away by welfare workers. A further two and a half years were added to David's other sentences. It now looked as if he would be spending most of the 1970s in prison.

Fairy Tale Romance

With David firmly behind bars, Catherine reluctantly moved on with her life. She accepted a position as a live-in domestic for a family in Fremantle and she fell in love with one of their sons.

It was a fairy tale romance with an elaborate wedding on Catherine's 21st birthday. Catherine soon gave birth to a baby boy, Donny. Her happiness came to an abrupt end seven months later, when she watched in horror as the child was crushed to death by a car.

Although five more children followed, the marriage was not happy. Catherine's thoughts increasingly turned to David and in 1983 she began seeing her old boyfriend again. David was also experiencing an unhappy marriage. After two years of sometimes not so clandestine meetings, Catherine picked up the telephone and told her husband that she was never coming back. And she kept her word.

David and Catherine then divorced their respective spouses. The reunited couple never married, but Catherine took David's name.

David had been obsessed by sex in his adolescent years. Now in his early thirties, his early compulsions had returned to him in full force. It was a Birnie family failing. His brother James had gone to prison for assaulting his six-year-old niece.

'She led me on,' was his defence.

While it does not appear that David was similarly attracted towards young girls, he did have some rather unconventional tastes.

He quickly found others who shared his interests. Soon, he was hosting group encounters at the couple's modest home. Catherine eagerly took part in these orgies.

David Birnie is led from court in handcuffs, 11 February 1987.

The couple were always looking for new sexual experiences and by 1986 they began discussing the abduction and sexual assault of young women. David told Catherine that she would experience intense orgasms when she saw him raping another woman.

On 6 October 1986 they kidnapped a pretty 22-year-old psychology student named Mary Neilson. She first met David at his place of employment, a Myaree scrap yard, on the outskirts of Perth. Mary needed tyres for her car and David told her that he had just what she was looking for at his home. When Mary crossed the threshold at 3 Moorhouse Street, she was threatened with a knife before being gagged and chained to a bed. David raped the woman repeatedly while Catherine watched. She even asked him questions about the experience.

After David had tired of Mary, he took her to Gleneagles National Park, where he raped her one last time. He then used a nylon cord to strangle her. When the girl was dead, David made a point of stabbing her. He mistakenly believed that the body needed to be perforated in order to allow gases to escape as it decomposed. Mary was then buried in a shallow grave. Six days after Mary had gone missing, her car was discovered in a car park that was directly across the street from Perth Police Station. David had driven it there himself.

Their second victim, 15-year-old Susannah Candy, was abducted, raped and murdered on the same day, 20 October. Susannah had been walking along the highway when the couple had picked her up. Once in the car, she was bound and gagged at knifepoint.

Chained to a Bed

Like Mary Neilson, Susannah was chained to a bed at the Birnie home and then raped. This time, however, Catherine joined in. When they had finished, the couple tried to strangle the girl, but she fought back and they found it hard to keep her down. During the struggle they managed to force sleeping pills down their victim's throat. When the medication took effect, David put a cord around Susannah's neck and then asked Catherine to prove her love for him by killing the girl.

Catherine had no problem with fulfilling David's request.

'I didn't feel a thing,' she said later. 'It was like I expected. I was prepared to follow him to the end of the earth and do anything to see that his desires were satisfied. She was a female. Females hurt and destroy males.'

David and Catherine buried Susannah in the national park, close to Mary's remains.

On the evening of 1 November, 12 days after the abduction and murder of Susannah Candy, the Birnies were on the prowl for another victim.

They spotted a woman standing by her car on the shoulder of Canning Highway. Noelene Patterson, a 31-year-old bar manager, had run out of fuel on her drive home from work. In need of a lift, she readily got into the Birnies' car.

The abduction of Noelene upset the dynamics at 3 Moorhouse Street. Taken by his captive's beauty, David kept putting off her murder. Catherine's feelings of insecurity rose to the surface as the days passed.

At one point she took a knife and threatened to stab herself through the heart unless David chose between them.

Their original plan had been to kill Noelene within hours of her abduction, yet here she was three days later very much alive. However, time was running out for the bar manager. Catherine's nagging, tears and threats all had their effect. David forced sleeping pills down Noelene's throat and then he strangled her as she slept. When they buried the body with the others, Catherine made a point of throwing dirt into the dead woman's face.

The next day, David and a very relieved Catherine were back on the road looking for their next victim. They found one in 21-year-old Denise Brown, who was walking home from visiting a friend. Her fate matched those of the Birnies' previous victims.

Corpse in the Back Seat

By this time, the couple had devised a fixed method of abduction. The victim would be lured into the car and threatened with a knife before being tied and gagged. However, they were not always successful. On the day after they abducted Denise, they offered a lift to a young university student as she was walking home from her classes. The offer was turned down because the girl wanted the exercise. As the Birnies tried to change the girl's mind, she noticed a person slumped in the back seat. She seemed to be sleeping.

It was Denise Brown. She was being driven to her death.

After the Birnies had failed to lure the university student into their car, they drove to a nearby pine plantation. Once there, David raped Denise twice. He stabbed her in the neck during the second assault, but when he stood up Catherine handed him a larger knife – she was not convinced that their captive was dead. Holding a flashlight, she looked on as David stabbed Denise repeatedly.

When he had finished, they prepared yet another shallow grave. But Denise was not dead. As the Birnies began to cover up what they thought was a corpse, the terrified girl sat up. David was stunned, but the shock was not enough to prevent him from grabbing an axe and striking his victim yet again. He hit the girl with all the force he could muster, but she sat up again just as the couple had gone back to burying her. This time, David brought the axe squarely down on her head, which split the young woman's skull in two. In the end, Denise Brown was buried just like the others.

Three days after Denise's grisly death, on the evening of 9 November, David and Catherine abducted their fifth victim, a 16-year-old girl whose identity is protected. She would bring their killing spree to an end. Her early hours at 3 Moorhouse Street matched the horrors experienced by the other victims. She was raped repeatedly as Catherine watched.

Next morning, Catherine untied her after David had left for his

Catherine Birnie leaves the Supreme Court in Perth after being sentenced to spend the rest of her life in jail.

DAVID AND CATHERINE BIRNIE

job at the scrap yard. She was then forced to telephone her parents. Catherine told her to tell them that she was staying with friends. Shortly afterwards, Catherine left the room to deal with someone who had arrived at the front door. She returned to find that her captive had escaped through an open window. Before the morning was over a number of police officers were standing outside the Birnie house.

There was no one there, so they waited. Catherine was arrested on kidnapping charges as she arrived home and David was picked up at his job.

Both of them denied kidnapping the girl. They insisted that she had willingly accompanied them to 3 Moorhouse Street in order to take the drugs they had offered.

David admitted having sex with her, but he continued to claim that the act was consensual. He stuck to his story through many hours of questioning. At the same time, he denied having anything to do with the recent spate of missing girls and women.

When David finally admitted the truth, it was in an unexpected way. The afternoon had passed and the evening was setting in, but no progress had been made. Suddenly a detective came out with a half-joking statement.

'It's getting dark. Best we take the shovel and dig them up.'

'Okay. There's four of them,' came David's reply.

After learning that David had confessed, Catherine too began to speak. She gave an explanation for her sloppiness in allowing the girl to escape earlier in the day:

'I think I must have come to a decision that, sooner or later, there had to be an end to the rampage. I had reached the stage when I didn't know what to do. I suppose I came to a decision that I was prepared to give her a chance... I had a great fear that I would have to look at another killing like that of Denise Brown, the girl he murdered with an axe. I wanted to avoid that at all costs. In the back of my mind I had come to the position where I really did not care if the girl escaped or not.'

It was 35 days after the first murder and Catherine was weary of the killings.

On 10 February 1987 David was taken to the Perth Supreme Court, where he pleaded guilty to the murders of Mary Neilson, Susannah Candy, Noelene Patterson and Denise Brown. He was sentenced to life imprisonment.

He last saw Catherine on 3 March, the day of her sentencing. The pair stood holding hands when Catherine learned that she too would be spending the rest of her life in prison. Although they were denied visiting privileges and telephone calls, David and Catherine kept in close contact by writing thousands of letters to each other.

The Outcome

In the early hours of 2 October 2005, David Birnie was found hanging in his cell. He was 55 years old. It was the day before he was due to appear in court on charges of raping a fellow prisoner.

Catherine was denied permission to attend his funeral. She applied for parole in 2007, but this too was denied. Two years later, Catherine Birnie earned the distinction of being the third woman in Australia to have her documentation flagged 'NEVER TO BE RELEASED'.

ALTON COLEMAN AND DEBRA BROWN

A convicted killer awaiting execution on Death Row once remarked that state executions are nothing more than legalized murders, but the families of the victims might disagree. Those who lost their loved ones to depraved killer couple Alton Coleman and Debra Brown in 1984 might consider their death sentences to be justice duly served.

Predictably, the pair exploited the United States appeals procedure to prolong the inevitable for as long as possible, asking for clemency from the State despite having offered none to their helpless victims. It is not only those who died at their hands who can be called their victims but also those who survived and are now traumatized for life. And then there are the bereaved families who now see the world as a cruel and dangerous place. What makes their grief even harder to bear is the fact that robber and rapist Alton Coleman was able to stay on the streets, even though the authorities knew he was a menace to society.

As a boy growing up in Waukegan, just north of Chicago, Coleman had been taunted by the local children, who called him 'Pissy' because he frequently wet his trousers. He was the African-American son of a prostitute who entertained her customers while he played in the same room. But his mother sent him to live with his grandmother when he became a burden to her. The experience warped his emotional development and contributed to his desire to dress in women's clothes and find gratification in rough sex. He also exhibited antisocial behaviour and was arrested for vandalism and acts of indecency throughout his teens. But he presented such a plausible personality in court that he managed to charm the judge and jury time and again.

Evading Justice

In 1973 he and a friend abducted and raped an elderly woman, but before the case reached court she was threatened by Coleman and did not press charges, so he was only indicted for robbery. After his two-year stretch he raped another woman but again escaped prosecution for that crime. As before, he was sent down for a less serious offence. Four years later he was free again and shortly afterwards he was charged with yet another rape. But he evaded a stiff sentence once again. A year later the whole charade was repeated. Each time he was accused of a serious sexual assault or robbery with violence he cited the earlier cases which had not been proven. By this means he raised a reasonable doubt in the mind of the jury, resulting in a nominal sentence for a lesser crime.

What the court did not see was Coleman's sinister side, for he was an insatiable sexual predator who could turn violent if crossed. He routinely threatened witnesses, and forced them to retract their statements on more than one occasion. In 1983 his own sister made a formal complaint against him after he had tried to rape his 14-year-old niece, but shortly afterwards she dropped the charges without explanation. In dismissing the case the judge observed that the mother was clearly 'terrified' of her brother, but without her testimony there was no case to answer.

The Killing Spree Begins

A year later, Coleman was accused of the rape and murder of a Chicago girl. She was the daughter of a former friend of his. Coleman must have known that the mother would not be intimidated into keeping silent, so on 2 June 1984 he fled the city with his girlfriend Debra Brown before he could be arrested. Brown had been diagnosed as a 'dependent personality'. She had been interviewed by the police the day before and would have warned Coleman of the seriousness of the charges hanging over him. He now knew that he was a hunted man and that his luck had run out. With a federal warrant out for his arrest and a witness who would not be cowed, he and Brown hid out for a fortnight before beginning their five-state crime spree. It was to last eight weeks and it involved one of the most intense manhunts ever mounted in America.

Their first victims were two young sisters, Annie and Tamika Turks, who were snatched off the streets of Gary, Indiana in broad daylight. The decomposing body of seven-year-old Tamika was found on 19 June. She had been strangled. Nine-year-old Annie survived a sexual assault, but was severely traumatized after witnessing the vicious murder of her sister. Coleman killed her by jumping on her face and chest until he had punctured her internal organs. It was this and similar acts of brutality that horrified even the most hardened detectives assigned to the case.

A week after Tamika Turks was found, Mr and Mrs Palmer Jones of Dearborn Heights, Michigan were attacked, beaten and robbed in their home. Coleman and Brown were identified as their assailants and as the thieves who had stolen the couple's car. Then on 5 July Coleman and Brown drove into Toledo, Ohio, where they talked their way into the home of Virginia Temple and her children. When they left, Virginia and her eldest daughter, nine-year-old Rachelle, were dead. They had been strangled. Anxious relatives found the surviving children huddled together and praying that the bad man and his girlfriend would not find their hiding place. Just hours later, Coleman and Brown broke into the home owned by Frank and Dorothy Duvendack, where they bound them with the telephone cable and stole money, valuables and their car.

Coleman was an insatiable sexual predator who could turn violent if crossed; Brown was a 'dependent personality'.

That afternoon Reverend and Mrs Millard Gay of Dayton, Ohio welcomed two new members to their congregation. Coleman affected his most disarming smile and Brown kept quiet as she played the dutiful girlfriend. While they enjoyed the hospitality of their hosts, the two fugitives listened patiently to an impromptu sermon on the rewards of helping one's neighbours. On 10 July the Gays' good deed even extended to giving the couple a lift to Cincinnati, thus evading the dragnet that had been set up to capture America's most wanted criminals. Then on 11 July an abandoned car belonging to 25-year-old Donna Williams, a resident of Gary, Indiana was found in Detroit. Nearby lay her body. The cause of death was strangulation. Coleman was the last person to have been seen with her.

The couple's next stop was Norwood, Ohio where on 13 July they posed as the potential buyers of a camper van that had been advertised for sale. While discussing the purchase Coleman brained the owner, Harry Walters, with a candlestick and then strangled his wife, Marlene. Mr Walters miraculously survived to identify his wife's killers, who had beaten the poor woman over the head more than 20 times, crushing her skull to fragments. The forensic evidence linking Coleman and Brown to the crime scene was irrefutable.

Two days later, the Walters' car was found in Kentucky. Coleman and Brown had once again swapped vehicles, this time for one owned by Kentucky college professor Oline Carmichael Jr. The professor was bundled into the boot of his car before being driven back to Dayton, where he was eventually found alive but in a state of shock.

One can only imagine the reaction of Reverend Gay and his wife when their lost sheep turned up at the door brandishing loaded guns and demanding more hospitality, but this time without the sermon. Coleman gave his hosts an assurance.

'I'm not going to kill you, but we generally kills them where we go.'

To the Gays' relief, Coleman and Brown left soon afterwards without resorting to their usual murderous violence. But they took Millard Gay's car and doubled back towards Evanston, exchanging it for another one en route, after killing the elderly driver.

The End of the Line

On 20 July 1984 the couple's merciless murderous spree ended quietly in their home town of Waukegan, Illinois without a shot being fired. A former neighbour recognized Coleman as he and Brown crossed the street and he telephoned the police. The couple were surrounded as they sat in a local park and they were taken into custody still protesting their innocence.

The police were presented with an open and shut case. No confessions were needed. The forensic evidence was compelling and there were a number of surviving eyewitnesses. Coleman would not be able to threaten them all. The only problem facing the authorities was deciding where to hold the trial, because the crimes had taken place in six states. In the end 50 law enforcement officers from the affected states held a strategy meeting, at which Ohio was chosen. United States attorney Dan Webb explained their decision to the press.

'We are convinced that prosecution [in Ohio] can most quickly and most likely result in the swiftest imposition of the death penalty against Alton Coleman and Debra Brown.'

To the dismay of his surviving victims Alton Coleman was able to stave off his execution for 16 years by invoking every constitutional loophole that his legal team could exploit. He claimed to have been represented by 'ineffective counsel', that the jurors at his trial were racially biased and that he suffered from an abusive childhood and a personality disorder. When these arguments failed he instructed his lawyers to protest that his rights would be violated by having his execution broadcast over closed-circuit television. But he was only delaying the inevitable. On the morning of 26 April 2002 46-year-old Coleman was strapped to a gurney in the death chamber at the Southern Ohio Correctional Facility near Lucasville and given a lethal injection consisting of three different chemicals, which sent him into oblivion. Among those who witnessed his exit was Harry Walters, whose wife Marlene had been beaten to death.

Brown had her death sentence commuted to life imprisonment on account of her low intelligence level and her master–slave relationship with the domineering Coleman. But she remained unrepentant. During her trial she sent the judge a note. 'I killed the bitch and I don't give a damn. I had fun out of it.'

MARLENE OLIVE AND CHARLES RILEY

In the spring of 1975, 16-year-old Marlene Olive was writing love poems to her adoptive parents while she got high on LSD on the campus of Terra Linda High School in Marin County, California. A few months later, she would douse their dead bodies with kerosene and set them alight after her love-struck boyfriend, 19-year-old Charles 'Chuck' Riley, had killed her mother with a claw hammer and shot her father. Marlene's grisly method of disposal led to the killings becoming known locally as 'the barbecue murders'.

It was a case that aroused a considerable amount of controversy because Marlene was tried as a juvenile, so she received a nominal sentence, whereas 'Chuck' was arraigned as an adult and sentenced to death. This was later commuted to life when the California Court of Appeal ruled that the death sentence was unconstitutional.

Riley's lawyer argued that his client was literally under Marlene's spell at the time of the slayings. He was a shy, insecure and impressionable teenager who had been hypnotized by a manipulative and unbalanced girl, who knew that her lover was uncommonly susceptible to suggestion. The court listened to recordings of Riley undergoing hypnosis by several professional therapists to demonstrate how easily he fell under their influence.

'He Was Lying'

But chief prosecuting attorney Josh Thomas dismissed this as mere showmanship. 'If I'd had the slightest doubt of Chuck Riley's guilt, I never would have taken the case,' he told a reporter. 'Under hypnosis, a subject talks in the present when recalling accurately. My expert pointed out that in critical testimony, Riley talked only in the past tense; therefore he was lying.'

Others disagreed. Jill Weissich, the daughter of Riley's attorney William Weissich, had the opportunity to study Marlene at close quarters in court. 'Marlene was definitely not your perky blonde cheerleader type. I had a chance to look into her eyes; she could've cast a spell on a lot of men.'

Riley's neighbours and classmates remembered him as a 'nice boy' who took to wearing black and changed for the worse after he came under the influence of 'wicked' and 'awful' Marlene Olive. But Marlene's counsel, Peter Mitchell, saw things differently. 'Both Marlene and Chuck were heavily involved in drugs and bizarre sex, and she fantasized about lots of things, possibly even killing her parents. But Chuck carried it out. He killed them both.'

Mitchell's faith in his client must have evaporated when he learned she had escaped from Ventura School, the low-security youth detention centre outside Los Angeles, only weeks before her release. It appears that she hustled her way to New York, where she worked as a prostitute to pay for her increasingly demanding drug habit.

In 1981 a reporter tracked her down and persuaded her to agree to a face to face meeting with her former lover, then doing time at the San Luis Obispo prison. The contrast between the two was striking. Marlene was ravaged by drug abuse and directionless, whereas Riley had become fit through a rigorous self-imposed exercise scheme and had educated himself to degree level. There was an awkward silence at first and then Riley started a long monologue about life in jail.

Marlene was shocked at how well he had coped without her, while she had deteriorated. When Riley finally paused and asked her what she was thinking, she had little to say. 'I'm thinking about all that has gone down. I guess we just lost our marbles.'

JAMES MILLER AND CHRISTOPHER WORRELL

When James Miller recovered from the car crash that had killed Christopher Worrell and their companion Deborah Skuse in February 1977, he did not mourn his deceased friend. Miller's overwhelming feeling was one of relief. Now the killings would end and he would be free of Worrell's malevolent influence.

The three had been holidaying at Mount Gambier, one of Australia's favourite beauty spots, when Worrell complained that he was having another manic depressive episode. He then demanded that they drive back to Adelaide. Worrell was at the wheel when a tyre blew. Losing control, he sent the car into a roll that catapulted all three occupants into the road.

Miller was the only survivor. Quite quickly he decided that no good at all would come of telling the police that his friend had been a serial rapist and killer and he did not feel the need to confess to his own part in the crimes. The more he thought it through, the more he convinced himself that he had been an unwilling accomplice, a victim, the only one to survive.

But he did not keep his terrible secret for long.

On 25 April 1978 ramblers found a severed leg in scrub near Truro in South Australia. Most of the flesh had been eaten by wild dogs, or had fallen away, but a shoe and some painted toenails had survived. A search of the area recovered clothes and more human remains, which forensic experts were able to identify as belonging to 18-year-old Veronica Knight, who had been reported missing from her home in Adelaide just before Christmas two years earlier. But there were no clues to her killer's identity.

Then a year later the remains of another teenage girl were found near the same site. These were identified as those of 16-year-old Sylvia Pittman, who had been reported missing at about the same time as Veronica Knight.

Now the police were certain that they were on to a serial killer, so they dug deeper into the missing persons' files and discovered that five more young women had disappeared in the area at around the same time.

The remains of two of these girls, Connie Iordanides and Vicki Howell, were soon located near the spot at which the first girl had been found, but neither of their corpses yielded clues that might lead to the arrest of their killer.

Funeral Confession

It was only after these discoveries were reported in the newspapers in May 1979 that a former girlfriend of Christopher Worrell came forward and claimed the reward for naming him as their killer and Miller as his accomplice. She told police that at Worrell's funeral she and Miller had been discussing Worrell's mood swings. When she revealed that Worrell had been diagnosed with a blood clot on the brain, Miller thought it might explain his dead friend's violent outbursts and his compulsion to murder any girl who resisted him. He allegedly confided his thoughts to her.

'It was getting worse lately. It was happening more often. It was perhaps a good thing that Chris died.'

When she was asked why she had not reported this at the time, she said she thought Miller's confession might have been a symptom of his own mental instability. Also, if Worrell was dead there was little point in naming him as a serial rapist and murderer.

But the bereaved families needed to know who had murdered their daughters and so did the police. They grilled Miller, now a homeless middle-aged drifter. After initially denying all knowledge of the killings, he confessed to having taken part in seven murders, three of which the detectives had not been aware of. He admitted that he had been Worrell's lover in prison, where the latter had been serving time for armed robbery and rape, and that on their release they had lived together in what Miller described as a dominant and submissive relationship. But Worrell soon tired of his slave and was impatient to practise his deviant behaviour on women, preferably innocent, unwilling ones so he could get a thrill from their humiliation and distress. He was then in his early twenties and was considered handsome, so he had no trouble in picking up single girls from clubs, bus stops and shopping malls. Some might even have felt safer after seeing his friend Miller sitting in the passenger seat. In any case, serial killers were almost unheard of at that time in Australia.

Each time Worrell had the urge to rape and kill he would stop the car at a lonely spot and Miller would make himself scarce until he could be certain that the deed was done. On a couple of occasions he claimed to have returned to see Worrell tie a girl up and then strangle her. He also said that he once tried to save one of the girls, but Worrell fought him off. But if he thought his story would convince the police to discount him as an accomplice, he was deluding himself.

James Miller stood trial for all seven murders in March 1980 and was found guilty on six counts of aiding in a criminal conspiracy. He was sentenced to six terms of life imprisonment. His lawyer argued that his client had not taken part in the actual killings and that he had no idea his former lover would kill the girls they had picked up, but the judge made it clear in his summing up that Miller must have known the likely outcome and that walking away from the murder did not absolve him of responsibility. The fact remained he had been present when each girl was enticed into the car and he had assisted in the disposal of the bodies.

Miller was due for parole in 2014, but he died from cancer on 21 October 2008. He was 68 years old.

ARCHIBALD HALL AND MICHAEL KITTO

Prior to his death in September 2002, Archibald Hall had the unenviable distinction of being the oldest person in Britain serving a life sentence. It was not the honour he had been hoping for.

Hall was born into a working-class district of Glasgow on 17 June 1924, the eldest of three children. By his own admission he had enjoyed a conventional upbringing and had performed well at school. However, he had a passive-aggressive personality that manifested itself in periodic outbursts of violence, the most notable being the occasion on which he had held a knife to his father's throat in an argument over a jacket. Hall evidently resented his lowly origins and was determined to prove himself the equal of the wealthier residents of the city, whom he secretly envied. He began by reinventing himself as a well-educated, softly spoken young man, which enabled him to con his way into middle-class households under a variety of pretexts, with a view to pocketing whatever he could. He also bamboozled the local Red Cross into allowing him to act as a collection agent, for which he used two tins – one for small change and the other for larger donations, which he kept for himself.

A sexually precocious youth, he had a voracious appetite for both genders and boasted of having had a series of casual male lovers by the age of 15, as well as an affair with an older woman, who gave him a taste of the lavish lifestyle he hungered after. The discovery that he was bisexual led to his decision to leave Scotland for the bright lights of London, where he thought he might be less conspicuous. There he successfully blended into the gay community, where he passed himself off as a wealthy American. He also ingratiated himself with the upper strata of society, enriching himself in the process. However, his plans did not go as smoothly as he had hoped. Shortly after moving south he was caught attempting to sell stolen jewellery and was given a stiff prison sentence. But his incarceration provided him with a unique opportunity to spend hours in the prison library, where he researched the subjects that would prove profitable in the profession he planned to pursue on his release – that of butler to the rich and famous. While the other inmates paced their cells or stared at the walls, Hall read everything he could on the subject of antiques and etiquette.

A 'Gentleman's Gentleman'

On his release he adopted the name Roy Fontaine and found a position as a 'gentleman's gentleman' to a member of the English aristocracy, which gave him ample opportunity to make an inventory of the silverware and other valuables. Hall's greatest assets were his dapper appearance and his carefully cultivated air of respectability, which immediately put prospective employers at their ease. He simply looked and acted the part to perfection. He was also acutely aware of how much store the aristocracy set by servants who knew their place, and so he was suitably deferential. This gave his victims the impression that he could be trusted. But beneath his veneer of cordiality Hall had no respect for the upper classes and his crimes could be seen as his way of making them pay for what he perceived as their arrogance.

Hall was a hedonist, a power-seeker who was driven by a need to avenge himself on a society from which he believed himself to be excluded. He was not a typical serial killer, but he was a psychopath.

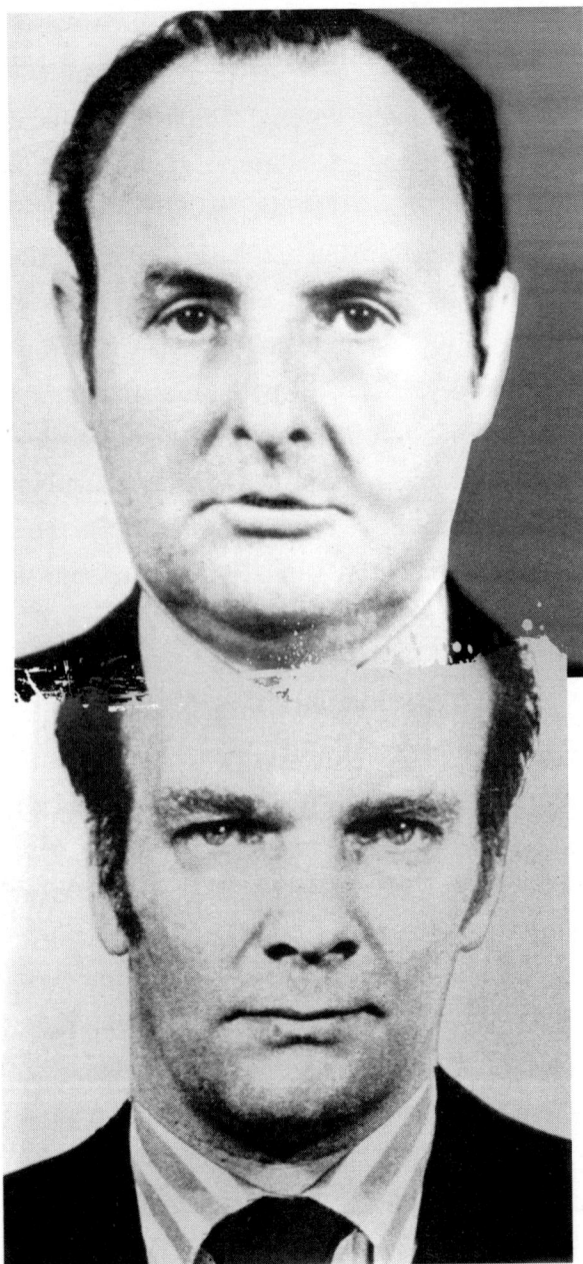

Hall (above) reinvented himself as a well-educated, softly spoken young man; Kitto was a petty thief.

If his own story is to be believed, he had no history of having suffered abuse at home or at school, where he had earned good grades. He had not exhibited any tell-tale traits such as cruelty towards animals, nor had he drawn attention to himself through aberrant behaviour. It was simply that he was an opportunist thief who would kill to cover his tracks because he was desperate to avoid being exposed as a criminal. Such a situation would have been entirely at odds with his own self-image of socialite and consummate actor. But although he was a convincing conman he was not a lucky one and before long he had once again been detained at Her Majesty's Pleasure, having been caught red-handed selling stolen property.

He returned to Scotland after his release in 1975 and despite his criminal record he managed to find work as a butler to Lady Hudson in Dumfriesshire. His intention had been to rob her, too, but he realized that he liked the dowager and his duties too much to risk losing them and he seriously considered 'going straight'. All might have ended well for Hall at this point, but unfortunately a former male lover and cellmate, David Wright, had obtained a job on the same estate. He threatened to expose Hall to his employer if he dared prevent him from helping himself to the old lady's jewels. Hall's solution was to lure Wright into the woods on the pretext of making him an offer to buy his silence and then shoot him in the back of the head with a gun used for hunting rabbits.

But Hall knew that even his silver tongue would not be able to convince the police that it had been a hunting accident, so he buried the body and submitted his resignation before he could be summarily dismissed.

His next job took him back to London where he used Lady Hudson's name to secure the position of head butler to the elderly Walter Scott-Elliot, a former Labour Member of Parliament, and his wife Dorothy.

A Fatal Partnership

Hall took the first opportunity to bring his lover and accomplice Mary Coggles into the household as a cleaner. She in turn introduced Hall to petty thief Michael Kitto, who proved the perfect foil for the avaricious conman. Kitto was a subservient, colourless individual whose fawning admiration for Hall's schemes fed his warped ego. Together the trio planned the robbery they hoped would set them up for life. But Mrs Scott-Elliot returned home early and demanded to know why her butler was showing a stranger around her home. Before Hall could offer an explanation Kitto had subdued the old lady by smothering her with a pillow.

Hall was just a career conman with convictions for nothing more serious than burglary and the chances were that Wright's murder would have remained undetected. However, he had made the fatal mistake of falling in with an unstable homicidal criminal who had now embroiled him in a second killing.

As they struggled to put the body to bed in an effort to make it appear that the woman had died in her sleep, her elderly husband awoke. Hall, however, kept his head and reassured the old man that all was well. Mrs Scott-Elliot had suffered a nightmare and he was putting her back to bed, so the old man could go back to sleep. The next morning Hall and Kitto cooked up a plot. They would sedate the husband and then drive up to Cumberland, where Hall had rented a holiday cottage. On the way, they would dispose of Mrs Scott-Elliot's body, which would be bundled into the boot. Mary Coggles would be persuaded to sit next to the old man, wearing his wife's wig and fur coat, for the benefit of any witnesses.

With that accomplished, Hall and Kitto returned to the scene of the crime and ransacked the house before travelling north again, where they tried to finish off the husband by strangling him. But he fought hard for his life so they beat him to death with a shovel and buried him at another remote location.

Dangerous Liability

By this point Mary Coggles had become a dangerous liability. She had insisted on keeping the murdered woman's jewellery and furs and had boasted to friends of her part in the affair. So Hall killed her too, caving in her skull with a poker and suffocating her with a plastic bag, before dumping her body under a bridge. The discovery of her corpse on Christmas Day 1977 did not, however, lead to the capture of the odd couple. It was the killing of their next victim, Hall's stepbrother Donald, that was their undoing.

Donald was a paedophile who had recently been released from prison. Having nowhere else to go, he invited himself to his brother's holiday home in Cumbria. He asked too many awkward questions, though, so Archibald and Kitto rendered him senseless with chloroform and then drowned him in the bath. But instead of burying him nearby Hall and Kitto decided to take the body to Scotland in the boot of their car and then dispose of it. It was an unnecessary risk and one which cost them their freedom. Before they reached their destination the weather worsened and they were forced to stay overnight at a hotel in North Berwick, where the landlord's suspicions were aroused by their odd behaviour. He was worried that the pair might try to leave the next day without paying their bill, so he decided to call the police, who checked the number plates on their car.

When they were found to be false, two uniformed bobbies were dispatched to the hotel. The car was searched and the body was found in the boot. Hall and Kitto were immediately arrested, but Hall managed to escape through a bathroom window during a break in the interrogation. He was soon recaptured in a nearby town.

The two men were tried twice – once in England and once in Scotland – for the five murders. Hall was found guilty of four of them, with the killing of Mrs Scott-Elliot set aside for legal reasons, while Kitto was convicted of three murders and sentenced to serve a minimum of 15 years.

The English judge told Hall that there was no possibility he would ever be released. With no hope whatsoever of freedom, he attempted suicide on several occasions but was unsuccessful. In 1999 he published his autobiography and called it *A Perfect Gentleman*, presumably with irony rather than in earnest.

KENNETH BIANCHI AND ANGELO BUONO

What do you say to the distraught parents of a young murder victim? This was the dilemma faced by Los Angeles homicide detective Bob Grogan when the parents of 20-year-old honours student Kristina Weckler came to identify their daughter's body at the county morgue in November 1977. Grogan had a teenage daughter of his own so he could imagine how the Wecklers must be feeling.

Earlier that day he had visited Kristina's apartment in Glendale, where he looked at her belongings and leafed through her diary for clues as to the identity of her killer. But he found nothing, only the evidence of a life cruelly cut short, of hopes unfulfilled. It had made him angry. He could cope with the killings of hookers and junkies downtown – at least they knew the risks – but this was a 'nice girl', the daughter of middle-class parents, and she was not the first to die that year.

There had been three other female victims before Kristina: Yolanda Washington, Judy Miller and Lissa Kastin. They had all been strangled and their naked bodies had been left on the hillsides north-east of Los Angeles. And there would be more, no doubt about it, until the killers were caught.

The suspicion that there might be more than one person involved came from the fact that there were no drag marks at the site in Highland

Park and the foliage had not been crushed. Two men must have carried the body and then set it down on the grass.

Grogan promised Mr and Mrs Weckler that he would bring their daughter's murderers to justice. It was all he could do. They nodded but did not take it in. They had their daughter's belongings to pack and her funeral to arrange once the coroner had agreed to release the body. If they had registered his assurance, they did not respond. But he meant what he said and as he left the apartment that morning he silently vowed to keep his word.

From the dark bands around her neck, wrists and ankles it was clear that Kristina had been tied down and throttled. There were no track marks on her arms so she was not an addict, but there was bruising on her breasts and there were needle marks, betraying the fact that she had been tortured. Blood could be seen around the rectum, which indicated that sodomy had taken place, but tests made on semen found at the scene proved inconclusive. The primary perpetrator must be a non-secretor, someone whose blood group and DNA cannot be determined from their bodily fluids. An investigator's nightmare.

If Grogan had wanted a day to think things through he was not going to get it. That same afternoon his partner, Detective Dudley Varney, was summoned to the scene of a double murder just a mile away in Elysian Park. The bodies of two young girls had been found on a rubbish heap in an advanced state of decomposition. The ants were already at work. Again there was no disturbance of the ground, supporting the theory that there were two perpetrators. This was confirmed by several witnesses, who had seen the schoolgirls talking to a man sitting in the passenger seat of a two-tone sedan. The victims were later identified as 12-year-old Dolores Cepeda and 14-year-old Sonja Johnson.

The seventh victim was found on 23 November, near the Golden State Freeway. Jane King was 28 years old. She had been dead for a fortnight.

Killing cousins: Angelo Buono (above) and Kenneth Bianchi were very different characters with very similar interests.

Searching for a Lead

The investigation into what the press were now calling the Hillside Strangler (it was supposed that only one killer was involved) was made a priority. A 30-man unit from the Los Angeles Police Department (LAPD), Glendale Police Department and the sheriff's office pooled their resources and shared the few leads that they had. But they had nothing of significance to go on – certainly not enough to prevent the killers from committing an eighth murder.

Sensible Girl

Eighteen-year-old student Lauren Wagner lived at home with her parents in the San Fernando Valley. When she did not come home on the night of 28 November her mother and father assumed that she would be in later. Lauren was a sensible girl and they could trust her. But when she had not returned by the next morning her father became anxious. His anxiety gave way to panic when he looked out and saw his daughter's car parked across the street with the driver's door wide open. He ran to the neighbouring houses and asked if anyone had seen her. Beulah Stofer had seen something. Lauren's car had been parked outside her house and a noisy argument had brought Beulah to the window. Looking out, she had seen a young woman struggling with two men.

'You won't get away with it!' she had heard the girl shout.

Then the girl was hauled inside the men's vehicle and driven away. But the old woman told herself that it was probably a domestic squabble. It was only when she received a threatening telephone call the next day and saw Lauren's car in the daylight that she realized that it had been her neighbour's daughter. All she could remember when questioned about the incident was that there had been two men. One was tall with a pockmarked face and the other was older, shorter and of Latin appearance, with bushy hair. She had not thought to note down their number plate but she remembered that their car was dark with a white top.

That afternoon Detective Sergeant Grogan had to make out another crime scene report. Lauren Wagner's naked body had been found on a hillside at Mount Washington in Glendale. Her body bore the same ligature marks and punctures as the previous victim's, as well as burn patches on the palms of the hands.

Taunting the Police

Victims nine and ten were found in mid-December 1977 and February 1978, but neither body offered any more clues. The first corpse belonged to escort agency 'model' Kimberly Martin, who was dumped in Echo Park, and the second to Cindy Hudspeth, a clerk. She had been murdered on her way to her evening job at a local college. Cindy's corpse had been locked in the boot of her car which had then been pushed off the road and down a steep embankment at Angeles Crest.

It was as if the killers were taunting the police by dropping bodies almost on their doorstep. By this time Bob Grogan had been partnered with Detective Frank Salerno of the sheriff's department, but these two highly experienced officers could not get their teeth into a case that continually led to a dead end. Even the profilers could not offer more than a standard description of a single white male in his late twenties or early thirties, who was of average intelligence and was now cold and manipulative as a result of a brutal upbringing.

On reading the report Grogan sighed. 'All we got to do now is find a white male who hates his mother.' Someone had the bright idea of bringing in a psychic, but this added little to the profile other than the suggestion that they should be looking for two Italian brothers in their thirties.

It was not that far off the mark as it turned out, but at the time it did not provide a lead the investigators could follow.

And then the curtain rose on the second act.

The 'Friendly' Security Guard

Two university students, Karen Mandic and Diane Wilder, were reported missing in Bellingham, Washington on 12 January 1979. Karen's boss told detectives that she had told him about a part-time house-sitting job she had taken in the exclusive suburb of Bayside. It was such an unusual opportunity that Karen had told her boss quite a bit about the circumstances that led to the offer, including the name of the security guard and the firm he worked for. When questioned, the man denied knowing either of the girls and claimed that he had been at a meeting on the evening they had disappeared. But his story did not check out.

At that stage Bellingham's chief of police, Terry Mangan, had a hunch so he decided to take charge of the investigation himself. He went to the apartment that Karen and Diane had shared, where he found the address of the house in Bayside that the girls had agreed to look after. When the security firm searched their files they confirmed that the guard had been assigned to watch the property, but had taken a company truck for repair on the night in question. However, the workshop had no record of the truck being serviced on that date.

A wet footprint was then found in the house but there was no sign of the girls, so Mangan ordered his men to make discreet inquiries in the neighbourhood. He suspected a kidnapping and did not want to panic the abductors into killing the girls in order to cover their tracks.

Finally, a neighbour informed the police that a security guard had asked her to keep a watch on the house, but on the night the girls disappeared he told her to keep away. The alarm system was faulty, he said, and he did not want her to trigger it accidentally.

Now was the time to issue a description of the girls and their car to the media in the hope that someone might have seen them that night. The police were in luck. Someone had seen the girls' car, which had been abandoned in a remote area. Their bodies were found inside. They had been strangled and beaten. Chief Mangan immediately ordered that the security guard be brought in for questioning. His name was Kenneth Bianchi.

Unusual Suspect

Bianchi was a most unusual suspect. An amiable, handsome man with an apparently friendly disposition, he was well liked by his employer and was considered a real gentleman by his girlfriend, Kelli Boyd, who was the mother of their young son. But when the police delved into his background they came across a totally different person. He was the son of a hooker who had given him up for adoption at birth.

Perhaps as a result, the boy became overly dependent on his foster mother. In adulthood he remained immature and irresponsible and he was also a practised, pathological liar, who thought nothing of gaining Kelli's sympathy by telling her that he was terminally ill.

He was also fastidious about the way his women dressed and he was liable to erupt into a childish tantrum if a girlfriend disobeyed his explicit instructions. His strict Catholic upbringing had conditioned him to expect every woman he went with to act in a prim and proper fashion and when they expressed a mind of their own he would become furious.

If they left him, he felt betrayed. He desired women but despised them for making him feel that way. It was the classic mindset for a serial rapist and a killer of women.

The Would-be Cop

Bianchi longed to enrol in the police force, but he failed to pass the entrance exams and so he had taken to working as a security guard as the next best thing. It gave him the sense of authority and self-respect he craved and it also gave him an opportunity to steal any items that caught his eye. When the Bellingham police searched his apartment they found an Aladdin's cave of loot, which enabled them to hold him while forensics ran tests on fibres and hairs found on the two dead girls and in the house on Bayside. Pubic hairs from the girls were found inside the vacant house and Bianchi freely admitted that he was the only person who had access to the property, other than the neighbour he had told about the 'faulty alarm' on the night the girls went missing. Among the articles of jewellery they recovered were two items belonging to victims Kimberly Martin and Yolanda Washington. They had him nailed. All they needed now was a confession and the name of his partner. But Bianchi was so wrapped up in his own fantasy world that it was impossible to know when he was being candid and when he was being deceitful.

Fantasy World

When he was not strutting around in his uniform he could not resist the urge to pose as a psychologist and counsellor, so he had set himself up in business with a set of fake qualifications and a hired office. Fortunately, no one trusted him with their secrets so he gave it in soon afterwards.

But the ambition to be a policeman did not recede so easily. While the hunt for the Hillside Strangler was at its height Bianchi talked the LAPD into allowing him to ride along with the patrolmen as part of a community relations programme. But all he did that night was drone on about the killings. It should have sounded alarm bells with the officers, but they were presumably just glad to get rid of him at the end of their shift.

Bianchi had been living in Los Angeles at the time of the 1977 murders and the police had interviewed him about one of the killings in his apartment block.

But he made such a convincing witness that he was not questioned a second time. The reason that the killings stopped in 1978 and then started up again in Bellingham in 1979 was that Kelli moved there after they separated and Bianchi followed, hoping for a reconciliation.

Chief Mangan was aware of Bianchi's history so he thought it was probably worth contacting the LAPD to check on his movements at the time of the Glendale killings.

Detective Frank Salerno took the call and was able to confirm that Bianchi had been living in the same street as Cindy Hudspeth and Kristina Weckler at the time of their murders. He had then moved to the apartment where Kimberly Martin had gone to meet a client before she vanished.

The final piece of the puzzle fell into place after the Los Angeles police circulated a photograph of Bianchi to the media, with a request for information. Among the many responses was a call from a lawyer, David Wood, who claimed to have saved a girl from a prostitution ring run by Bianchi and his cousin, Angelo Buono.

The 'Italian Stallion'

Detective Grogan lost no time in tracking down Angelo so that he could grill him on his movements on the critical dates. He was accompanied on the drive down by Salerno's partner Pete Finnigan. They had a feeling that Buono was the right man the moment they met him. He was crude, hostile and clearly untrustworthy – a real thug. He was also antagonistic from the outset, on the defensive as soon as the cops mentioned that they were following up a lead on Becky Spears and Sabra Hannan, two of the girls from his prostitution ring. He had something to hide and it was a big ugly secret. The more they probed him for details and dates, the more aggressive and uneasy he became. He bared his crooked teeth in barely disguised contempt and ran his dirty fingers through his dyed black hair as he glared from one cop to the other and back again.

This was the self-titled 'Italian Stallion' who had called his mother a whore to her face and had abused his numerous lovers. He had been married several times, but he made no secret of his loathing for women, who found him primitively attractive until he had beaten them black and blue. Even as a teenager he had bragged of raping and sodomizing girls in the neighbourhood and he was a known admirer of serial rapist Caryl Chessman, who had passed himself off as a policeman to lure prostitutes into his car. Former girlfriends and wives had accused him of sexually abusing his own children and of threatening anyone who dared to leave him. And yet underage girls had been attracted by his cocksure arrogance and animal magnetism. It was one of the things that attracted his cousin Kenneth Bianchi to him in the autumn of 1975. Kenneth hoped he could pull the girls that hung around Angelo and maybe learn a few tricks from the big bad wolf. The first scam he learnt was how to get free sex from a hooker by flashing a fake police badge when the deed was done. The girls were out of the car and down the street before the cousins had stopped grinning.

'You can't let a c**t get the upper hand,' he told Bianchi. 'Put them in their place.'

Prostitution Ring

It was not long before they had the idea to work their own prostitution ring by recruiting teenage runaways and threatening them with violence if they objected or withheld their earnings. But then one of the girls met lawyer David Wood, who helped her to leave the city. Soon afterwards the second girl escaped. Angelo was not going to let Wood get away with derailing his gravy train, but Wood knew how to deal with thugs like Angelo. He sent one of his heavies round – a former client – who let the would-be pimp know that it would be in his best interests to let the girl go. Write her off as damaged goods, so to speak.

But Angelo was not a man to be pushed around or put off when he could smell easy money. So he roped his cousin into his next scheme, which was abducting a girl off the street and setting her up as their private prostitute. But first they had to invest in a list of 'Johns' who were regular customers of the girls that plied their trade on Sunset Boulevard. When the list turned out to be a fake they swore they would skin the hooker alive who sold it to them, but they could not find her so they abducted and killed her friend, Yolanda Washington, instead. And that is how the Hillside Stranglers started.

A Killer's Alter Ego

Once in custody Kenneth Bianchi was informed that the case against him was rock solid and that if he did not co-operate he would be facing the death penalty. Cornered, Bianchi resorted to an old trick from his childhood. He rolled his eyes up inside his head and pretended that he could remember nothing. When that did not get him the sympathy he was seeking, he faked a multiple personality disorder. He had been watching television in his cell when a movie on the subject had given him the idea. By the time an expert had been dispatched to test him, Bianchi had rehearsed his routine. It was a good enough performance to convince Dr John G. Watkins, but Detective Salerno had spotted the critical slips in Bianchi's story. On several occasions he referred to his homicidal alter ego, Steve Walker, in the third person instead of the first as if telling a story that had happened to someone else. If the disorder had been genuine he would have used 'I' and not 'he'.

Detective Grogan greeted the news with his customary wry humour. He told Salerno that he would ask the judge to set Bianchi free but send 'Steve Walker' to Death Row. That would give him something to work on. The detectives grew even more despondent when the court-appointed psychiatrist Dr Ralph B. Allison confirmed the diagnosis. Bianchi was not faking, he said. Then the prosecution brought in their own expert, Dr Martin T. Orne, who immediately contradicted his two colleagues. Dr Orne gave Bianchi a number of rigorous tests designed to rule out anyone who was shamming. He concluded that the subject was indeed faking.

But Dr Orne was not going to engage in a credibility contest with his colleagues. He knew that the court would weigh his conclusions against the two experts who disagreed with him and would most likely favour them, so he threw a wild card into the game. As he was packing away his papers he told Bianchi that it was very rare to find a subject who had only one personality squatting in his head. It was more common to find subjects tormented by three or more.

Bianchi took the bait just as Dr Orne had hoped. He created a second uninvited guest, who would share the blame for the killings with the fictional 'Steve'. Dr Orne's scepticism was shared by another independent expert, Dr Saul Faerstein, who had been called in by the prosecution to give a second opinion. With the odds now even, Bianchi was prepared to drop his act and listen to a one-time offer from the district attorney.

If he admitted his part in the Bellingham and Glendale murders and was prepared to testify against Angelo Buono he would get life, with the chance of parole at some unspecified future date. The death penalty would be off the table. It was an offer he could not afford to refuse.

The Cousins Stand Trial

Bianchi's confession was supported by photographic line-up identifications made by two eyewitnesses (Beulah Stofer, the elderly neighbour who had witnessed Lauren Wagner's abduction and Markust Camden, who had seen the kidnapping of Judy Miller). In addition there was compelling forensic evidence. Material found on the bodies of Judy Miller and Lauren Wagner was peculiar to Angelo's home and upholstery workshop, a place where he worked alone. And the rabbit hairs found on Lauren's corpse matched the pets that Angelo kept. Together this was enough to secure an arrest warrant for cousin Angelo.

Detectives are trained to be impartial and objective so that the evidence decides the guilt or innocence of a suspect. It is imperative that they are non-judgmental when interviewing someone accused of a particularly vile crime. If they betray a hint of revulsion, they risk the suspect clamming up. But on 22 October 1979 Detective Sergeant Bob

Grogan could not mask the deep satisfaction he felt when he handcuffed Angelo Buono and read him his rights. Grogan would readily admit that it would take a far more forgiving man than he was to have treated the murderer of Kristina Weckler and at least nine other women with impartiality (Buono was finally convicted of killing eight people).

Like so many criminals, Angelo was stupid beyond belief. After the well-publicized arrest of his cousin he had not thought to dispose of his wallet, which betrayed the imprint of the fake police badge with which he had conned the prostitutes. But just when the investigation team was congratulating itself on a job well done, Kenneth Bianchi pulled another infuriating stunt.

He got cold feet at the thought of testifying against his cousin, which would have made him an informer, so he retracted his confession and named another man. It was someone he had obviously dreamt up in an effort to sidetrack the police and cast doubts on his own culpability.

Bianchi played the confused, mentally unstable witness to the best of his ability when he was called to the stand on 6 July 1981, but the judge was having none of it. His contempt for the witness was only several degrees higher than his disdain for the district attorney, who had moved to have the case dismissed for fear his conviction record would be spoiled by an acquittal.

Judge George ruled that dismissal would not be 'in the furtherance of justice... nor is it the function of the court automatically to rubber-stamp the prosecutor's decision to abandon the People's case.'

District Attorney Kelly had been warned. The charges against Angelo must be made and answered before a jury. Politics had no place in the courtroom. Smarting from his public reprimand the district attorney withdrew, forcing the attorney general to appoint four special prosecutors to consider the strength of the case against Buono. Their decision was unanimous. Buono must answer the charges.

After numerous delaying tactics the case finally came to court in

November 1981, but Bianchi was still playing the prima donna. Then the judge reminded Bianchi that he was within his rights to send him to a more Spartan institution if he violated the conditions of his plea bargain by changing his story. From then on he played ball. But the case did not hinge on Bianchi, even if he believed it did. During the two-year trial more than 250 witnesses placed Buono at the scene of the crimes and testified to his sadistic impulses.

On 31 October 1983 the foreman of the jury handed the clerk of the court the jury's first verdict. It related to the murder of Lauren Wagner. There could be no doubt. It was guilty. There followed eight more guilty verdicts and only one not guilty. The murder of Yolanda Washington could not be proved.

Buono had the nerve to protest that his rights had been violated, but no one was listening. For reasons known only to itself the jury voted to spare Buono from the death penalty, which angered Judge Ronald George, who reminded them of the seriousness of the charges.

'Angelo Buono and Kenneth Bianchi subjected various of their murder victims to the administration of lethal gas, electrocution, strangulation by rope, and lethal hypodermic injection. Yet the two defendants are destined to spend their lives in prison, housed, fed and clothed at taxpayer expense, better cared for than some of the destitute law-abiding members of our community.'

Buono spent the first part of his sentence in Folsom Prison, where he refused to come out of his cell in case other inmates imposed their own brand of justice on the woman-beater. He died in Calipatria State Prison on 21 September 2002, apparently from a heart attack.

Tainted Love

Only one personality type is more disturbing and incomprehensible than a multiple murderer and that is the serial killer 'groupie'. Some of them are deluded women who have convinced themselves that they can redeem a tortured soul through love while others, their even more psychotic sisters, share the predator's perverse desires.

Kenneth Bianchi attracted one such admirer, who offered to make the ultimate sacrifice to procure his release. Wannabe writer and actress Veronica Compton struck up a correspondence with Bianchi during his trial by claiming that she needed his opinion on her play *The Mutilated Cutter*, which concerned a female serial killer.

As their strange 'relationship' intensified through prison visits and voluminous letters, Veronica suggested that she could murder a girl in the same manner as the Hillside Strangler and then dump the body in the same area as the most recent killings. That would make it appear that the real killer was still at large, forcing the authorities to declare her lover innocent. She would even be prepared to smuggle a sample of his semen out of the prison and smear it on the victim.

Veronica was arguably certifiable, but she was not a proficient killer. She needed copious amounts of booze and cocaine before she could summon up enough courage to go through with the scheme and even then she bungled it badly. After talking a young woman into driving her back to her motel in Bellingham she attempted to strangle her with a cord, but the woman fought her off and escaped. Veronica caught a flight back to California before the police arrived, but the cocktail of cocaine and alcohol she had consumed intensified her mental problems, which tipped her over the edge. She became hysterical and was later arrested in connection with a garbled anonymous letter she had sent to the LAPD, in which she claimed that Bianchi was innocent. As proof, the letter drew their attention to the botched murder attempt in Bellingham.

When detectives investigated the motel incident the intended victim gave them a detailed description of her female assailant, which they matched to the hysterical woman at the airport.

Veronica was jailed for attempted murder, but her passion for sex killers was as ardent as ever. She lost interest in Bianchi and turned her attentions to multiple murderer Douglas Clark [see p.145].

During an exchange of Valentine cards he sent her a photograph of a headless corpse as a love token. She returned the gesture by scribbling a note.

'I take out my straight razor and with one quick stroke I slit the veins in the crook of your arm. Your blood spurts out and spits atop my swelled breasts. Then later that night we cuddle in each other's arms before the fireplace and dress each other's wounds with kisses and loving caresses.'

And she wondered why no one had wanted to stage her play.

Despite her failure to sabotage Bianchi's trial she offered to testify on his behalf. She told a convoluted story about a conspiracy to implicate Angelo, but it did not make sense. It was evident she was using the opportunity to get publicity for herself. She did not deny she had talked of opening a mortuary in partnership with Clark so that they could have sex with the dead and she was candid about the other perverse pleasures they were planning if he was ever released. Then she was drawn into admitting her part in trying to lay a false trail by strangling the woman in Bellingham. By the end of the session even Kenneth Bianchi must have been grateful to go back behind bars.

MARIO FURLAN AND WOLFGANG ABEL

Some people can be too clever for their own good. When an uncommonly high level of intelligence is combined with an oversized ego, money to burn and time to kill, a potentially lethal cocktail is created. Add in a fatal psychological flaw – the inability to tell the difference between right and wrong – and the mixture becomes explosive. If such people have been raised on the idea that their privileged background sets them above the law, it will only be a matter of time before they test their 'superior' intellect against the simple deductive reasoning practised by the police.

Italian Mario Furlan and his German friend Wolfgang Abel were the sons of wealthy parents. Like their predecessors Leopold and Loeb, whose crime formed the basis of Alfred Hitchcock's *Rope*, they thought it would be fun to see if they could outwit the authorities in a game of murder.

Mario was 26 years old and his friend was 27 when in August 1977 they decided to make their morbid fantasies a reality by setting a drug addict on fire and blaming it on a fictional neo-Nazi named 'Ludwig'. This was the first in a series of apparently random killings by the pair. Furlan and Abel targeted individuals whom they despised for reasons known only to themselves.

Both had everything that money could buy. Abel lived a life of luxury in the family home in the exclusive Verona suburb of Monte Ricco (Mountain of the Rich). His father was a former managing director of a West German insurance company. Furlan's father was a plastic surgeon whose income had bought a beautiful house in the suburbs of the city. But both young men were described as strange and isolated by their former classmates and fellow university students.

'Ludwig' Strikes Again

The murder of the drug addict was followed by the fatal stabbing of a casino employee in Padua, the brutal beating and knifing of a homosexual writer in Venice, the axe murder of a prostitute and the killing of two priests in Vicenza. The priests were bludgeoned to death with hammers.

Another priest was later murdered when a nail was hammered into his head and a chisel was embedded in his brain. And in Verona a hitchhiker was burned to death while he slept, unable to free himself from his sleeping bag. Then five people died in an arson attack on a pornographic cinema in Milan.

The police were baffled. The killings were committed in different towns, the methods were dissimilar and there appeared to be nothing to link them other than the enigmatic letters that were left at each scene. Written in Italian, they were signed by the mysterious 'Ludwig'.

Each note was headed with a swastika and each bore a slogan such as 'We are the last Nazis'. But there was no forensic evidence with which to identify the writer and there was a considerable gap between incidents. Added to that, the random nature of the attacks made it impossible to predict where or when the killer, or killers, might strike next.

'Framed'

The police had their answer on the evening of 3 March 1984, when Abel and Furlan were caught attempting to set fire to furniture in a crowded disco near Mantua. When the friends' homes were searched, evidence was recovered linking Abel to the letters.

The pair's trial began on 1 December 1986 and it lasted until January. At its conclusion, each man was handed a 30-year sentence. Doubts as to their sanity saved them from a life in prison, but it was all academic because they were released soon afterwards for reasons which remain unknown. Critics of the Italian judiciary claim that their freedom was bought and paid for while others cite the judge's compassion for two young men who were clearly not in their right mind at the time of the murders. And there are some who say that the judges were uneasy at the idea of condemning men purely on the basis of circumstantial evidence. Only Furlan and Abel knew the truth. The pair were given house arrest in the small villages of Mestrino and Casale di Scodosia in Padua, where they spent their days in idleness. In the years afterwards, both welcomed the chance to tell the story of how they were 'framed' for the crimes perpetrated by the elusive 'Ludwig'. In October 2024, Abel died at the age of 65.

CAMERON AND JANICE HOOKER

Cameron Hooker seemed like a pretty regular guy. He was slightly gawky-looking and not particularly intelligent, but he was no dummy either. The most you could say about Cameron was that he was good with his hands. It was a skill that would enable him to pursue his fantasies and bring about a seven-year nightmare for one very unfortunate young woman.

Cameron was born in 1953 in the small Californian city of Alturas, though he spent much of his youth in the marginally larger community of Red Bluff. An unremarkable student, he began working at a local lumber mill while attending high school. He spent much of the money he earned on the sort of pornography that was produced for those with a leaning towards sadism and masochism. Cameron kept his fantasies secret until the age of 19, when he met Janice. Four years his junior, she was a plain, shy, insecure high school girl with little experience of the opposite sex. Cameron believed that he had found someone who could be moulded to fulfil his desires. After a period of polite dating, he introduced Janice to a series of violent sexual acts, which involved bondage, flogging and near-asphyxiation.

In 1975, two years into the relationship, Cameron married Janice. However, even at the wedding, he had begun to tire of his teenage bride.

Her submissive nature did not quite fit his fantasies. What Cameron wanted was a sex slave. And Janice? What did she want? Janice wanted a baby.

The young couple struck a bargain. Janice could have her child if Cameron could have a sex slave. Throughout his wife's pregnancy, the lumber mill worker built a number of wooden boxes, each of them designed to confine a victim and muffle their cries for help. Cameron went about his preparations with great care, all the while making sure that no one could see what was going on at the rented Red Bluff house. Such was his dedication that the arrival of the couple's child – Janice's child, really – did little to alter his plans. Cameron would not be rushed – everything had to be just right.

It was not until several months after the birth that Cameron went out and got his slave. Janice went along for the ride. Indeed, it might be said that she was used as a lure. Who would suspect a woman with a baby in her arms?

The woman that Cameron would call his slave was Colleen Stan, an attractive 20-year-old from Eugene, Oregon. On the morning of Thursday 19 May 1977 she left her home to visit a friend in Westwood, California, some 500 miles (800 km) to the south.

It did not worry Colleen that she had no car and little money, because she considered herself an experienced hitchhiker. By the middle of the afternoon the young woman had travelled nearly 350 miles (560 km) to Red Bluff, just an hour and a half west of her final destination. Colleen's arrival in this small Californian community marked the beginning of the final and most challenging leg of her trip. Up until this point, she had been travelling along the busy Interstate 5 (I-5), where rides were plentiful, but now she had to use the less-travelled State Route 36, which would take her into Westwood.

With the end of the journey in sight, the seasoned Colleen continued to show great caution, turning down the first two offers of rides. The third car to stop was Cameron's blue Dodge Colt. When she realized that the smiling man at the wheel was accompanied by a mother and child, all of her fears melted away. But Colleen gradually began to feel uneasy. She noticed that Cameron constantly stared at her through the rear-view mirror.

Under normal circumstances this type of warning sign would have prompted her to look for a way out. In fact, when the car stopped at a service station Colleen sought refuge in the toilets and considered escaping.

'A voice told me to run and jump out a window and never look back,' she later recalled.

But then there was the wife and the baby – surely the leering young man would not do anything with them around.

So Colleen returned to the car, unaware that she would not be free again for a long time. Just moments after pulling away from the service station, the Hookers talked about making a quick visit to some nearby ice caves. Cameron turned the Dodge on to a dirt road and after several minutes he brought it to a halt. The Hookers and their baby got out of the car, but Cameron returned. Jumping into the back seat, he pointed a knife at Colleen's throat. Terrified and fearing death, she allowed herself to be handcuffed, blindfolded and gagged. Cameron then locked a heavy, insulated plywood box around her head.

After Janice and the baby had returned to the car, Cameron turned it around and headed back to Red Bluff with his trophy – though he stopped for some fast food along the way. Once home, Cameron led Colleen into his basement, where he strung her up by the wrists before stripping off her clothing and whipping her.

Where was Janice in all of this? Presumably she was upstairs with the baby – though she came down to the basement to have sex with her husband as Colleen hung suspended in front of them. After the couple had finished, Cameron released Colleen's wrists and forced her into a coffin-like box. Then he once again locked the small plywood box around her head before leaving.

The initial horror that Colleen had experienced marked the beginning of a routine that consisted of whippings, beatings, choking, burning and electrocution.

When she was not being subjected to these tortures, Colleen was chained up in the larger of the two boxes. Eventually, Cameron constructed a small cell under the basement staircase, where he set his slave to work, shelling nuts and other menial tasks.

Weird Contract

After seven months had passed, Colleen was presented with a contract stating that she agreed to become Cameron's slave. Although it was just a simple piece of paper, the document marked the point at which Colleen's nightmare intensified. After he had forced her to sign the paper, Cameron told her that she had been registered with a body called 'The Slave Company'. It was a powerful organization, he claimed, whose operatives had the house under constant surveillance. Any act of disobedience would mean certain death for Colleen's relatives, he said.

Because she had signed the contract, Colleen – known simply as 'K' – was given access to the rest of the Hooker house. This meant nothing in terms of freedom. Instead, she was now charged with performing the household chores. Cameron continued to torture Colleen and he often interrupted her busy day to whip her.

Events soon took another dramatic turn when Cameron took Colleen into the master bedroom. However, any hopes he might have had of a *ménage à trois* were dashed when Janice refused to join in. Nevertheless, Cameron raped Colleen after his wife had left the marriage bed.

Things changed again when the family moved to a mobile home on an acre of land they had bought just outside Red Bluff. Having lost his basement, Cameron kept Colleen captive in a new box that slid under

Cameron Hooker kept his sex slave in a wooden box with the consent of his wife.

his waterbed. As Colleen lay in her box, the conception and birth of the Hookers' second child took place noisily above her.

Though Colleen spent more time in the box under the bed than in the coffin-like container at the old house, she was now allowed outside. She had contact with the neighbours and she even went jogging. It was only her fear of the Slave Company and what it might do to her family that prevented her from escaping.

Witnessing these examples of servitude, Cameron's confidence grew and his fantasies changed. In 1980, during the fourth year of captivity, he sent both his wife and his slave to a local bar to pick up men. When Colleen was not looking after the Hooker children, she was sent out into the streets of Reno and other communities to beg for money. Cameron's boldest move came when he had his slave write letters to her three sisters – they were the first signs they'd had that Colleen was still alive. Emboldened, he allowed a phone call and, eventually, a visit to her divorced parents in southern California.

On 20 March 1981, a thin, tired-looking Colleen was dropped off at her father's home. She had been gone for almost four years. It was a pleasant, if tense, visit. Little was said because her family were wary of driving her away. On the following morning, not long after she had attended church with her mother, Colleen was picked up by Cameron – or 'Mike' as he called himself. It was the name he had used three years earlier on the slave contract.

Back to Square One

Colleen's return to the mobile home in Red Bluff marked yet another change in her circumstances. In many ways, it was a return to the treatment she had known when she had first been taken captive. Cameron bothered with her much less and the torturing became less frequent.

Colleen's days were now spent almost entirely in the box under the waterbed. Deprived of exercise and daylight, her hair began to fall out and she lost more weight.

She listened as Cameron began talking to Janice about acquiring another slave – perhaps more than one. Cameron spent a good portion of the summer and autumn of 1983 digging a hole near the mobile home, so that a dungeon could be built. After he had installed flooring and walls, it became Colleen's home. However, the underground chamber soon flooded, so Colleen was returned to her box.

After that failed experiment, Cameron came to the conclusion that he needed to move to a bigger place before he abducted more slaves. In order to achieve his goal, he sent Colleen to work at the local King's Lodge Motel. The young woman remained dutiful, telling co-workers nothing of her situation. Yet it was at the motel that Colleen's chains of captivity began to loosen. On 9 August 1984, she was picked up from work by Janice. The car trip home was anything but routine. Janice told Colleen that there was no Slave Company, no one was watching the mobile home and the contract was bogus. In short, every threat Cameron had used to keep her in bondage was a lie.

Janice Hooker leaves court in Red Bluff, CA after giving testimony at a hearing.

The Torturer Weeps

That evening, the two women planned Colleen's escape. By the next morning Colleen was on a bus to southern California, having been wired money by her father. Before leaving Red Bluff, she telephoned Cameron from the station. He cried when she told him that she was leaving. There would be more telephone calls in due course.

Although Colleen had told no one about her seven-year ordeal, she could not leave the Hookers behind. It was not long before she began calling Janice on a regular basis. She made 29 telephone calls in total, in which she encouraged Janice to leave Cameron. Colleen had grown bolder since she had discovered the truth about the Slave Company and she stood up to Cameron whenever he answered the phone. In tears, he pleaded with her to come back. The tables had turned.

After one abortive attempt, Janice did leave her husband, after making a full confession to her church minister, Pastor Dabney, who then telephoned the police. On 18 November, the Hookers were arrested. There would, however, be only one trial because Janice had been granted full immunity from prosecution in exchange for agreeing to testify against her husband. It took over ten months for Cameron's case to come to trial. He testified in his own defence, arguing that all sex acts with Colleen had been consensual. On 28 October 1985, Cameron Hooker was found guilty of kidnapping, rape and eight other offences. He was sentenced to a total of 104 years in prison.

GERALD AND CHARLENE GALLEGO

In the weeks before Christmas the residents of Sacramento, California are out and about in the shopping malls and suburbs, rattling their collection tins to raise money for their favourite charities. In December 1980 the money they raised was in aid of a good cause but it was not for the homeless or the poor. It was to pay for the prosecution of a serial rapist and killer. When the county admitted that its diminished budget meant that it might not be able to afford to sustain proceedings against Gerald Armond Gallego, who had been accused of raping and murdering nine young women, the incensed citizens took their anger out on to the streets. They raised a total of $28,000 to ensure Gallego stayed behind bars until the case against him could be proven beyond all reasonable doubt.

Criminal Roots

Gallego's attorney argued that his client was suffering from post-traumatic stress disorder as a result of head injuries he had sustained as a child, which had left him brain-damaged. The condition had been compounded by extreme abuse at a tender age. He was therefore not responsible for his actions and he was not able to 'plan, problem-solve, comprehend or make judgements' regarding his own defence.

Whether any of this was true or not, 34-year-old Gerald Gallego had certainly been capable of planning and problem-solving when he had carried out a series of brutal sexual assaults and murders in California over a two-year period. According to Gallego he simply could not help himself because he was 'infected' with bad blood. His family on both his mother's and his father's side had allegedly been professional criminals and he was therefore genetically predisposed to be antisocial. Although this excuse was blatantly nonsensical, it was a matter of record that Gerald had been offending from an early age. He was just six years old when he was caught breaking into a house and 12 years old when he was placed in a young offenders' institution for 'lewd acts' with a six-year-old girl.

At the age of 15 he was arrested for armed robbery and on his release in December 1963 he not only continued to reoffend but he also married the first of five wives. All of them were said to have been beaten and abused by the man one of them called her 'Jekyll and Hyde'.

From Soulmate to Killer's Mate

Then in the autumn of 1977 Gallego met his soulmate at a poker club. She was an equally disturbed and violent person named Charlene Adell Williams, who was herself twice divorced. However, she soon had to put up with Gallego's abuse and beatings whenever he failed to satisfy her sexually – which was frequently. In her frustration she turned to another woman. Gallego went into a violent rage when he caught them sleeping together, but fortunately the girl escaped with her life. She was one of the luckier ones.

The depth of Gallego's depravity can be gleaned from the fact that he 'celebrated' his 32nd birthday by sodomizing his own daughter. She had allegedly been abused by him since the age of six.

Gallego's conscience was disengaged and his sense of right and wrong was severely impaired, to say the least. There was nothing and no one to prevent him from unleashing his predatory instincts on the real world. Apparently, though, Charlene did not need convincing. She was up for it too. So on 11 September 1978 they cruised the streets of Sacramento in their Dodge van in search of a sex slave. They couldn't believe their luck when they spotted two teenage girls – 17-year-old Rhonda Scheffler and 16-year-old Kippi Vaught – in a shopping centre. It was easier than they could ever have imagined. Charlene enticed the girls into the back of the van by inviting them to smoke pot and Gallego thrust a loaded revolver into their faces as soon as they were inside. He told them that if they screamed he would shoot them right then and there and then he ordered them to lie face down on the floor of the van so he could bind them with adhesive tape. Gallego drove to a secluded spot while Charlene watched over the girls and then he raped them over and over again. After that he drove to another remote area, where he untied them and ordered them outside. Finally, he shot them both at point-blank range.

Charlene and Gerald were married just over two weeks later, on 30 September 1978. But they did not hang around to celebrate their nuptials because the groom's daughter had filed charges against her father, accusing him of incest and unlawful intercourse. They fled to a hotel in Houston, Texas where Gerald signed in as Stephen Robert Feil.

But Gerald could not contain his bloodlust for long so on 24 June 1979 he ordered Charlene to drive to a nearby county fair, where he hoped to find another unwilling victim. Charlene procured not one but two teenage girls – 14-year-old Brenda Lynne Judd and 13-year-old Sandra Kay Colley – by pretending that she needed help to distribute leaflets and was willing to pay for it. But in a terrible repetition of the first killings the girls were driven to a remote spot in the Nevada desert, where they were raped and murdered – only this time Gerald split their skulls with a hammer.

That autumn the couple moved back to Sacramento where Gerald, still using his alias, found a job as a barman. Then on 24 April 1980 the whole horror was repeated for the third time. Two teenage girls – 17-year-old Karen Chipman Twiggs and 17-year-old Stacy Ann Redican – were abducted in broad daylight.

Charlene had procured them by offering them some marijuana. The brutal pair buried them in shallow graves 20 miles (32 km) from Lovelock, where Gerald had killed them in a frenzied attack with a hammer. Gerald and Charlene got married for the second time on 1 June 1980, in an effort to legitimize their alias. Six days afterwards, they abducted 21-year-old Linda Aguilar, who was four months pregnant at the time. Linda was hitching on the highway and she assumed that she would be safe with a married couple, but she was raped, beaten with a rock and left for dead. The pathologist who later performed the autopsy concluded that she had been alive when she had been placed in the hastily dug hole and that in her efforts to crawl free she had pulled in the sand that had suffocated her.

Fatal Mistake

So far the duo had abducted strangers but on 17 July 1980 Gerald commemorated his 34th birthday by kidnapping a girl he knew. Thirty-four-year-old barmaid Virginia Mochel was forced into the van as she walked home from the tavern where she worked as a barmaid. She was raped and strangled and then her body was left in undergrowth near Clarksburg.

By now the couple were over-confident and ripe for making a fatal mistake. Eight people had been killed and they had not even been questioned once by the police. They had got away with it and it seemed likely that they would continue to do so, but on 2 November Gerald got cocky and careless. He changed their routine by deciding to abduct a young couple in broad daylight and without using Charlene as bait. After striding up to 22-year-old Craig Miller and 21-year-old Mary Sowers in the street he forced them into the vehicle at gunpoint, in full view of their friends.

Charlene had to put up with Gallego's beatings when he failed to satisfy her and she took a female lover.

Their friends had not seen the gun or they would have called the police right away, but they made a note of the vehicle's licence plate. It seemed strange that Craig and Mary should get into a van owned by a man they had never seen before. They thought they knew all of Craig and Mary's friends and it just did not look right. However, they did not act on their suspicions – there might have been a rational explanation. But when the couple did not return after a few hours their friends called the police and gave them the licence number. It was already too late for Craig and Mary. Gerald killed Craig before taking Mary back to his apartment, where he raped her while Charlene looked on. She was pregnant at the time and unable or unwilling to have sex with her husband, so she did not object to him satiating his lust with another woman. The couple then drove the girl to a lonely spot where Gerald shot her three times.

Evading Execution

When the police arrived at the couple's apartment they made a cursory search of their vehicle. They quickly found several spent bullet casings, a few reels of duct tape and some restraints, which gave them sufficient grounds to arrest the Gallegos and impound the van.

Charlene did not stand by her man but gave him up on the advice of her attorney, who struck a plea bargain for her. She was sentenced to 16 years and eight months in prison on condition that she would never be extradited to answer charges in any other state. Charlene's testimony secured Gerald's conviction for the murder of Mary Sowers and Craig Miller, for which he was sentenced to death in June 1983. In June of the following year he received a second death sentence for the killing of Karen Twiggs and Stacy Redican, but that sentence was to be ruled invalid 14 years afterwards. The judge had apparently prejudiced the jury by telling them that Gallego might eventually be paroled if he escaped execution.

In March 1999 Gerald instructed his lawyers to appeal against the remaining death sentence on the grounds of insanity. He began to exhibit erratic behaviour such as sleeping under a table in his cell and complaining that people from the 'dark side' were after him.

While Gallego continues to draw out the appeals process in a desperate attempt to impede the wheels of justice, the citizens of Sacramento are satisfied that they contributed in some small way to his incarceration. Ask any one of them and they will tell you that it was money well spent.

DOUGLAS CLARK AND CAROL BUNDY

Doug Clark and Carol Bundy appeared to make an unlikely couple. Doug was a good-looking man from a well-to-do family, a 32-year-old charmer with a string of girlfriends pining after him. Carol was a divorcee with thick glasses and a weight problem. Five years older than Clark, she had recently split from an abusive husband and was working as a nurse. Underneath, however, the pair had a great deal in common: both were sexually driven, both lacked a moral compass and together they embarked on a rampage of sexually motivated murder.

'King of the One-night Stand'

Douglas Daniel Clark was born in 1948, the son of a Naval Intelligence officer, Franklin Clark. The family moved repeatedly during Doug's childhood, due to his father's work. He later claimed to have lived in 37 countries. In 1958, his father left the navy to take up a civilian position as an engineer with the Transport Company of Texas: some sources suggest that this was in fact merely a cover for continuing intelligence activities. Either way, it did not put a stop to the family's nomadic lifestyle. They lived in the Marshall Islands for a time, moved back to San Francisco, and then moved again, to India. For a while Doug was sent to an exclusive international school in Geneva. Later, he attended the prestigious Culver Military Academy while his father continued to move around the world. When he graduated in 1967, Doug naturally enough enlisted in the air force.

At this point, however, Clark's life began to unravel. He was discharged from the air force and for the next decade he drifted around, often working as a mechanic, but really concentrating on his vocation as a sexual athlete: 'the king of the one-night stand' as he liked to call himself. The 70s was the decade when casual sex first became a widespread, socially acceptable phenomenon – at least in the big cities – and Doug Clark, a smooth-talking, well-educated young man, was well placed to take advantage of this change in the nation's morals.

Nowhere was this lifestyle more prevalent than Los Angeles, and eventually Doug Clark moved there, taking a job in a factory in Burbank. One of the bars he liked to frequent and pick up women was a place in North Hollywood called Little Nashville, where, in 1980, he met Carol Bundy.

Bundy was 37 years old. She had had a troubled childhood: her mother had died when she was young, and her father had abused her. Then, when her father remarried, he had put her in various foster homes. At the age of 17, Bundy had married a 56-year-old man; by the time she met Clark she had recently escaped a third marriage to an abusive man, by whom she had had two young sons. Most recently, she had begun an affair with her apartment block manager, a part-time country singer called John Murray. She had even attempted to bribe Murray's wife to leave him. Murray's wife was not pleased at this and had told her husband to have Bundy evicted from the block. However, this had not ended the infatuation and Bundy continued to show up regularly at venues where Murray was singing. One of these was Little Nashville.

Clark, an experienced manipulator of women, quickly saw the potential in seducing the overweight and transparently needy Bundy. He turned on the charm and won her over immediately. Before long, he moved into her apartment and soon discovered that this was a woman with whom he could share his increasingly dark sexual fantasies.

Prostitutes

He started bringing prostitutes back to the flat to have sex with them both. Then he began to take an interest in an 11-year-old girl who was a neighbour. Carol helped lure the girl into sexual games and posing for sexual photographs. Even breaking the paedophile taboo was not enough for Clark, however. He started to talk about how much he would like to kill a girl during sex and persuaded Carol to go out and buy two automatic pistols for him to use.

Clark was always the picture of a charming and confident man in court.

The killing began in earnest during June 1980. In June, Clark came home and told Bundy about the two teenagers he had picked up on the Sunset Strip that day and subsequently murdered. He had ordered them to perform fellatio on him and then shot them both in the head before taking them to a garage and raping their dead bodies. He had then dumped the bodies beside the Ventura freeway, where they were found the next day. Carol was sufficiently shocked by this news to make a phone call to the police admitting to some knowledge of the murders but refusing to give any clues as to the identity of the murderer.

Twelve days later, when Clark killed again, Bundy had clearly got over her qualms. The victims were two prostitutes, Karen Jones and Exxie Wilson. Once again, Clark had picked them up, shot them and dumped the bodies in plain view, but this time he had decided to take a trophy: Exxie Wilson's head. He took the head back to Bundy's house and surprised her by producing it from her fridge. Almost unbelievably, she then put make-up on the head before Clark used it for another bout of necrophilia. Two days later, they put the freshly scrubbed head in a box and dumped it in an alleyway. Three days after this, another body was found in the woods in the San Fernando Valley. The victim was a runaway called Marnette Comer, who appeared to have been killed three weeks previously, making her Clark's first known victim.

Clark waited a month before killing again. Meanwhile, Bundy was still infatuated with John Murray. She would go to see him singing in Little Nashville, and after a few drinks her conversation would turn to the kind of things she and Clark got up to. These hints alarmed Murray, who implied he might tell the police. To avert this, Bundy lured Murray into his van after a show to have sex. Once they were inside the van, she shot him dead and decapitated him. However, she had left a trail of clues behind her: Bundy and Murray had been seen in the bar together and she had left shell casings in the van. Bundy herself was unable to take the pressure. Two days later, she confessed to her horrified co-workers that she had killed Murray. They called the police and she began to give them a full and frank confession about her and Clark's crimes.

Clark was immediately arrested and the guns found hidden at his work. Bundy was charged with two murders: Murray and the unknown victim whose killing she confessed to having been present at. Clark was charged with six murders. At his trial he represented himself and tried to blame Bundy for everything, portraying himself as an innocent dupe. The jury did not believe him, and he was sentenced to the death penalty, while Bundy received life imprisonment. Ironically enough, it was Bundy who met her end first, dying in prison on 9 December 2003 at the age of 61. Clark, meanwhile, died in 2023 of cardiovascular disease while still sitting on death row in California.

ALVIN AND JUDITH NEELEY

Gravedigger John Hancock of Georgia considers himself one of the luckiest men alive.

On 3 October 1982 he and his fiancée, Janice Kay Chatman, accepted a lift from a young woman who shot him in the back and left him for dead and then sped off with his terrified companion.

After his recovery, Hancock learnt that he and Janice were the latest victims of a pitiless pair of serial killers who were suspects in a murder inquiry. The assassins were also sought for questioning in respect of two separate incidents – in the first one, shots had been fired at a victim's house and on the second occasion, another home in the same area had been firebombed. Hancock's miraculous escape proved to be the turning point for a case that had been confounding the Georgia police for a month.

While he was giving his statement at police headquarters, Hancock quite by chance overheard a recording of a threatening telephone call made by a young woman to the family who had been firebombed. He immediately identified the voice as that of the girl who had shot him and abducted Janice Chatman.

At first detectives were sceptical. It seemed incredible that Hancock and Chatman would accept a ride from a stranger simply because she said she was lonely and would appreciate their company. Their initial thoughts were that Hancock had invented the story to divert suspicion from his part in the disappearance of his fiancée and that he had sustained the bullet wound in a struggle. But his insistence that he had been shot by the woman who had made the recording – and the fact that his description of her car matched a description given by a witness in the firebombing incident – convinced police to take his evidence seriously. Furthermore, Hancock claimed that the woman had two young children in the back of the car, which had convinced Janice and him that she was genuine.

The 'Nightrider'

Hancock's story also contained further clues to the woman's identity and that of her unseen male accomplice. During the drive the woman had talked to a man over her CB (Citizens' Band) radio. She had called him the 'Nightrider'. John was a CB radio user himself and he noticed that the frequency she was using was too weak to reach someone she claimed was transmitting from the next state. He then became anxious when they drove out of town and a large intimidating figure approached the car. The man introduced himself as the Nightrider and told them to follow him to a spot where they could get some of the finest hooch in Georgia. By the time the two cars came to a halt Hancock had no idea where they were.

When he got out to relieve himself he realized that the young woman had followed him into the forest and was holding a gun to his head. She ordered him to walk off the path into the trees and then she fired, hitting him in the right shoulder. But she did not check that he was dead. When he heard the cars driving away he staggered down to the highway and flagged down a passing trucker who took him to hospital.

The bullet recovered from his shoulder was analyzed by ballistics and the descriptions of the two cars – a brown Dodge with white stripes and a red Granada – were noted in the case file, together with an artist's sketch of the duo, drawn to match John's description. It was at this stage in the investigation that the abduction of Janice Chatman, the ongoing murder inquiry and the two residential attacks converged.

Finding a Link

Detective Sergeant Kenneth Kines re-interviewed Linda Adair and Kenneth Dooley, the homeowners who had been subjected to the threatening phone calls, the arson attack and the shooting. They had both worked at the Youth Development Centre for troubled girls, so he asked them if any incident might have given one of the female inmates grounds to hold a grudge. They denied any suggestion of institutional abuse and repeated that they had nothing in common other than the fact that they had both worked at the YDC. They lived separate lives and could not think of any girl who might be targeting them.

But Detective Kines was convinced that there was a link. He trawled through the files at the YDC searching for a troubled teen who might fit the profile and before long he had narrowed the list down to five names. Among them was that of Judith Ann Neeley, whose physical description happened to match that given by Hancock and the other witnesses. Her file also contained the fact that she had been arrested for armed robbery and was familiar with firearms. When Linda Adair, the YDC worker whose home had been firebombed, heard that Janice Chatman's abductor had two children in tow she remembered that a young offender at the centre would have had two children of the same age. Her name was Judith Neeley. Adair had kept photographs of her and her husband Alvin, which she now passed to the police. When these were shown to John Hancock he identified Neeley as his attacker and her husband Alvin as the elusive Nightrider. The couple were being held in Tennessee on other charges, so it was simply a matter of asking the neighbouring state to have the suspects transported to Georgia, where they would take part in an identity parade.

Alvin and Judith were a lawless trailer trash couple with a record as long as the Mississippi, including hold-ups and car thefts from Georgia to the Mexican border. Judith's husband was 12 years her senior, a flabby hog of a man who was described by Detective Kines as 'a pathetic character if ever there was one'. Yet the 18-year-old Judith was devoted to him. In 1980 the pair were convicted of robbery and passing stolen cheques. Alvin went to prison for five years and Judith was detained at the YDC, where she gave birth to twins. While there, she alleged staff had sexually abused her. Perhaps she wanted attention. The police investigated but found no evidence to substantiate her claims, which only served to fuel her resentment.

The Children Were a Lure

Shortly after Judith's release in 1981 she was caught robbing a grocery store, but she wriggled out of a prison sentence on account of the twins. When Alvin was released six months later they had to take the children along with them wherever they went. So the children were in the back of the car when they sprayed YDC worker Kenneth Dooley's home with gunfire and threw a Molotov cocktail at Linda Adair's house.

The children were also used to lure 13-year-old Lisa Ann Millican into the car at the Riverbend Mall in Rome, Georgia, coincidentally the site of a robbery Judith had carried out two years earlier. While police searched for the girl in vain, they received three anonymous phone calls from a female who directed them to the site where the body could be found, but no corpse was recovered. More calls followed. This time there was a more detailed description of the location and a female officer at the YDC was accused of complicity in the crime. Clearly someone was out to implicate the centre, even to the extent of murdering an innocent young girl in order to cast suspicion on the staff. Whatever the caller's motive might have been, the police took the tip seriously and decided to search the area again more thoroughly.

Alvin and Judith Neeley were a lawless couple with a record as long as the Mississippi.

At nightfall on 29 September 1982 a search team spotted a girl's body at the bottom of a canyon. There was a single bullet in her back. She had evidently been murdered and had then been thrown 80 ft (24 m) to the rocks below. A pair of bloody jeans was found nearby, which did not belong to the victim, and three empty syringes were recovered from the scene. Back at the crime laboratory these syringes were found to contain traces of drain cleaner. It had been injected into the girl's neck, causing the fat under her skin to boil. The pain must have been excruciating. The victim, now identified as Lisa Ann Millican, had also been sexually assaulted. It later transpired that Alvin and Judith had kept Lisa chained to a bed in a hotel room, while Alvin raped her in the presence of their children. It was apparently his idea to kill her by injecting her with drain cleaner, but it was Judith who carried out the gruesome execution.

Six times she jabbed the needle into the screaming teen, until she realized that it was not going to prove fatal. It was then that she shot Lisa and pushed her over the edge on to the rocks below.

Within a week Judith was looking for a second victim. She failed to persuade a woman waiting at a payphone to accept a lift, mainly because the woman had just called her husband so that he could pick her up.

But the intended victim had also felt that there was something disturbing about Judith, which made her uneasy about accepting a ride.

It was shortly after this incident that Judith picked up John Hancock and Janice Chatman. When she had disposed of John, Judith rejoined Alvin and they drove Janice to a motel where they raped her repeatedly, then shot her and dumped the body in a creek. But before the couple could slaughter more innocents they were arrested for passing forged money orders in nearby Murfreesboro, where they were questioned by detectives who knew exactly who they were dealing with.

There was no let-up in the interrogation that turned the screws on the flustered Alvin. Finally he confessed to 15 murders, all of which he claimed had been instigated by his wife. She was a control freak, he said, and he feared that she would kill him if he double-crossed her. He laid all the crimes on her and she initially took the blame – or the credit as she would see it. But he was not entirely unco-operative. He drew detectives a map indicating the location of Janice Chatman's body, so he could not deny his part in disposing of the corpse.

The Bride of Frankenstein Syndrome

The evidence against Alvin was largely circumstantial in the case of Lisa Millican but it was strong enough to secure a conviction for the abduction, rape and murder of Janice Chatman. So the Tennessee district attorney decided to underwrite the risk by splitting the couple. He ordered the prosecutors in his own state to prepare the case against Alvin for the kidnap and murder of Janice Chatman, which would mean a statutory life sentence, but he extradited Judith to Alabama to be tried for the first degree murder of Lisa Millican, which carried the death penalty. She also faced two other counts of abduction with intent to terrorize and abduction with intent to harm.

An insanity plea was thrown out after Judith was deemed fit to plead by the Alabama state psychiatrist, so her attorney, Robert French Jr, fell back on the 'battered woman' defence. On the opening day of the trial at the DeKalb County Courthouse at Fort Payne in March 1983, French portrayed his client as a puppet controlled by her violent and abusive husband, who was not present to defend himself. In the ensuing days French called Alvin's first wife to the stand to testify to her husband's violent outbursts and the physical scars that she still bore.

Then Judith was sworn in. She described how she had committed the crimes under duress and at her husband's direction. Alvin had ordered her to kidnap girls for him to rape and she did not possess the will to resist. She had given Lisa the fatal injections of drain cleaner out of compassion, to end her suffering, but she had no idea that it would take so many to kill her.

The only anecdotal evidence to support her assertion came from John Hancock, who told the court that he had heard Alvin twice order her to hurry before she shot him. But the district attorney countered that Alvin had not ordered her to take him out and kill him. John Hancock had left the car to urinate and Judith had followed him into the forest on her own initiative. She then shot him when she could have let him escape if she had wanted to. The district attorney also succeeded in entering into evidence the letters that Judith had written to Alvin after their arrest. These contradicted the version of events that she was giving on the stand and under oath. Clearly she was a woman who would perjure herself and sacrifice her partner to save her own skin.

French made a last ditch plea for leniency by citing a psychiatric condition known as 'coercive persuasion', in which sufferers instinctively do what they are told because they have been conditioned to do so after being subjected to brutality and isolation. But the State's expert witness, psychiatrist Alexander Salillas, refuted the idea by saying that even battered women still had a choice. According to the examination which he had carried out, he said, Judith Neeley knew the difference between right and wrong and had made a conscious decision to commit murder.

When the jury retired on 21 March 1983 they spent the evening in deliberation and then returned a verdict the next morning. It was 'guilty on all counts'. It is thought that the jury recommended that Judith be sentenced to life imprisonment rather than death on account of her age, but the judge ruled that her actions betrayed a callous nature fully justifying the death penalty. Her crimes had been uncommonly cruel and many who attended the trial or who had been privy to her interrogations concurred that she had been the instigator and Alvin had been the duplicitous servant.

In March 1987 the United States Supreme Court rejected her appeal and two years later it upheld the death sentence. But before it could be carried out it was commuted to life imprisonment without parole by the then governor of Alabama, Fob James, who justified his highly controversial decision by saying that the jury had recommended that she serve life and that he felt duty-bound to honour their recommendation.

Neeley's tender years persuaded some to lobby for the reinstatement of her right to parole and in July 2002 Montgomery Circuit Court judge Gene Reese ruled that she could be considered for release but not until January 2014. However, even if she was granted parole in Alabama, the Tennessee district attorney's decision to try Judith and Alvin separately means that she could still stand trial in Georgia for the rape and murder of Janice Chatman.

The law may have its flaws, but it seems that it will not be mocked in the southern states.

LEONARD LAKE AND CHARLES NG

As individuals, Leonard Lake and Charles Ng were both unsavoury characters. Together, they were a deadly combination. In the space of little over a year, they killed, tortured and raped at least 12 and perhaps as many as 25 people, including men, women and two baby boys. The men were mostly killed for money; the women, for sexual thrills; and the babies simply for being in the way.

Leonard Lake was a fat old hippie obsessed with survivalism. Charles Ng was a young ex-marine from Hong Kong, with an addiction to stealing. What brought the two of them together initially was an interest in guns.

Evil Fantasy

The sexual enslavement of women had long been a fantasy of the older of the two men, Leonard Lake. Lake was born in San Francisco on 20 July 1946. His parents by all accounts had a dreadful relationship and, when Lake was six, his mother left, leaving him with his grandmother. As a child, Lake collected mice and enjoyed killing them by dissolving them in chemicals (a technique he would later use to help dispose of his human victims). In his teens, he sexually abused his sisters.

At 18, Lake joined the US Marines and made the rank of sergeant. He served two tours in Vietnam as a radar operator. Following a spell in Da Nang, he suffered a delusional breakdown and was sent home before being discharged in 1971. He was already married by this time, but his wife left him because he was violent and sexually perverted.

Unhealthy Obsession

Lake became part of the hippie lifestyle centred around San Francisco. He also became increasingly obsessed with the idea of an impending nuclear holocaust, and for eight years lived in a hippie commune near Ukiah, in northern California. There he met a woman called Claralyn

Leonard Lake custom-built a dungeon in the woods.

Balazs, or 'Cricket', as he nicknamed her. A 25-year-old teacher's aide when he met her, Balazs became deeply involved in Lake's fantasies. She starred in the pornographic videos he began to make, the latest manifestation of his sexual obsession. His other obsession was with guns – part of his survivalist paranoia – and through a magazine advert he placed in 1981, he met Charles Ng.

Born in Hong Kong, Ng, or 'Charlie' as Lake called him, was a disruptive child, obsessed with martial arts and setting fires. His parents sent him to an English private school in an effort to straighten him out, but he was expelled for stealing. Next, he went to California where he attended college for a single semester before dropping out. Soon after that he was involved in a hit-and-run car crash and to avoid the consequences he signed up for the US Marines, fraudulently claiming to be a US national. It was at this time that he met Lake. They came up with a plan to sell guns that Ng would steal from a marine arsenal. However, Ng was caught stealing the guns and was sentenced to three years in prison.

When he was released in 1985, he immediately contacted Lake, who invited him to his new place, a remote cabin near Wilseyville, California, that he was renting from Balazs. He had custom-built a dungeon next to the cabin ready for his friend Charlie to come up and have fun. It is thought that by then Lake had already murdered his brother Donald and his friend and best man Charles Gunnar, in order to steal their money and, in Gunnar's case, his identity.

Over the next year Lake and Ng indulged themselves in an orgy of killing, rape and torture. Their victims included their rural neighbours, Lonnie Bond, his girlfriend Brenda O'Connor plus their baby son Lonnie Jr, and another young family, Harvey and Deborah Dubs and their young son Sean. In both cases the men and babies were killed quickly, while the women were kept alive for Ng and Lake's perverse sport. They would rape and torture the women – Lake filming the whole awful business – before putting them to death. Other victims included workmates of Ng's; relatives and friends who came looking for Bond and O'Connor; and two gay men.

Their career of evil might have gone on a lot longer if it had not been for Ng's addiction to stealing. On 2 June 1985, Ng was spotted shoplifting a vice from a San Francisco hardware store, probably for use as a torture implement. Ng ran away from the scene. Lake then appeared and tried to pay for the vice. By then, however, the police had arrived. Officer Daniel Wright discovered that Lake's car's number plates were registered to another vehicle, and that Lake's ID, in the name of Scott Stapley, was suspicious. When Wright found a gun with a silencer in the trunk of the car, he arrested Lake. Once in custody, Lake asked for a pen, paper and a glass of water. He then wrote a note to Balazs, and quickly swallowed the cyanide pills he had sewn in to his clothes. After revealing his true identity and that of Ng, he went into convulsions from cyanide poisoning and died four days later.

Kilos of Bone

Further investigation soon led the police to the Wilseyville ranch. Ng was nowhere to be seen. However, they found Scott Stapley's truck and Lonnie Bond's Honda there and, behind the cabin, they found the dungeon. Officers noticed a human foot poking through the earth, and proceeded to unearth 18 kg (40 lb) of burned and smashed human bone fragments, relating to at least a dozen bodies. (A month or so later, less than a mile away, they were to find the bodies of Scott Stapley and Lonnie Bond, stuffed into sleeping bags and buried.) They also came across a hand-drawn 'treasure' map that led them to two five-gallon pails buried in the earth. One contained envelopes with names and victim IDs suggesting that the full body count might be as high as 25. In the other pail, police found Lake's handwritten journals for 1983 and 1984, and two videotapes that showed the horrific torture of two of

Charles Ng - shoplifting was to be his downfall.

their victims. If there was any doubt that the missing Ng was as heavily involved as Lake, it was dispelled by these tapes, that showed Ng right there with Lake, even telling one of the victims, Brenda O'Connor: 'You can cry and stuff, like the rest of them, but it won't do any good. We are pretty – ha, ha – cold-hearted, so to speak.'

Ng, meanwhile, was on the run. He had flown to Detroit and crossed the border into Canada where he was eventually arrested. In a Canadian prison, he began an epic legal battle against extradition back to the United States on the grounds that Canada did not have the death penalty, and thus to send him back to the US would be in breach of his human rights. It was not until 1991 that he finally lost this battle and was shipped back to the States. Even that was not the end of the story. Ng managed to stretch out pretrial proceedings for another seven years at the astronomical cost to the state of $10 million. Finally, in May 1999, some 15 years after his crimes, Ng was convicted of murder and sentenced to death. To no one's surprise, Ng appealed against the verdict.

THIERRY PAULIN AND JEAN-THIERRY MATHURIN

Some individuals never come to terms with their sexual identity and prefer to blame others for the confusion and guilt that it brings them. Guyana-born transvestite Thierry Paulin blamed his grandmother for the neurosis that drove him to murder 21 elderly women in the Parisian district of Montmartre between 1984 and 1987. His lover, Jean-Thierry Mathurin, from Martinique, played an active part in the torture of nine of the victims to please his partner and to earn a share of the cocaine with which they celebrated each slaying.

The victims were all found bound, gagged and beaten in their homes before being strangled, suffocated or smothered. One had been force-fed caustic soda and another had been stabbed 60 times. This told the police that they were hunting a psychotic individual who was re-enacting the same revenge scenario over and over again. The victims' homes were then ransacked in a search for cash and jewellery, which indicated that the killer must have had an accomplice – it was unlikely that someone in a violent rage would have been capable of such rational behaviour. The torture of the victims was his primary motive.

But Paulin and Mathurin had already left the city when the Paris police rounded up every sex offender they could find. They were living the high life in Toulouse, where they snorted coke and partied in the most exclusive gay clubs in town. Then like all thieves they fell out, leaving Paulin to return alone to the capital where he was soon arrested for a violent assault on a drug dealer. He was released from prison in 1987, before he had served his full 16-month sentence, when he resumed his killing spree. But one elderly victim lived long enough to give the police a good description. She told them her attacker was a black man with dyed platinum blond hair and large earrings. When Paulin was arrested on 1 December he immediately broke down and confessed, but he was not going to go down without taking his old partner and lover with him.

The trial gave him the attention and recognition he craved. He appeared in court dressed like a garish imitation of Norma Desmond, the deranged silent movie queen in the film *Sunset Boulevard*. But his days in the spotlight were numbered. He died of AIDS on 16 April 1989, before his guilt could be proven beyond doubt.

Paulin (above and in drag) died before he could be sentenced; his accomplice Mathurin got life, but was freed in 2009.

JAMES MARLOW AND CYNTHIA COFFMAN

As the privileged daughter of a St Louis businessman, Cynthia Coffman enjoyed the good life, but she was forced into a loveless marriage when she became pregnant at the age of 17.

Her devoutly Catholic parents refused to let her have an abortion and they threatened to cut her off without a cent if she did not marry before the neighbours noticed her condition. But after five years of domestic tedium Cynthia left her husband and young son to hit the highway. She had no plans, other than to get as far away as she could from the life she loathed. When she ran out of fuel and options in Page, Arizona she did what all unqualified young women in smalltown America would do – she took a job as a waitress in a diner. She then met a local man and moved into his apartment, but they were evicted shortly afterwards when the neighbours complained about their drunken behaviour.

In May 1986 the couple were arrested for speeding during a road trip to California and Cynthia's boyfriend was jailed for six weeks for possessing an unlicensed gun. It was while she was visiting him in prison that Cynthia set eyes on her boyfriend's cellmate – bad boy James Gregory Marlow – and decided that she wanted to change partners. Marlow, who was 29 years old, had convictions for robbery with violence, burglary and car theft. He also had delusions of his own superiority and wore tattoos of the neo-Nazi Aryan Brotherhood with pride.

'I Belong to the Folsom Wolf'

Cynthia was not there to meet her boyfriend when he was finally released from jail. She and Marlow were on their way south to fleece Marlow's family of all they could beg, borrow or steal. It was not long before his relatives got wise to them and sent them packing, forcing the couple to sleep rough in the woods, where they doused themselves with petrol to keep the ticks off. Within days Marlow was back to breaking into houses and making off with petty cash and any weapons he could lay his hands on. That July they were married. The nuptials were sealed in an unusual way, with the bride having her buttocks tattooed with the inscription, 'I belong to the Folsom Wolf'.

But that autumn their criminal careers took a nasty turn when they kidnapped and murdered 32-year-old Sandra Neary in Costa Mesa, California. Sandra's car was found abandoned in a local car park, where she had gone to withdraw money from a cash machine. Two weeks later her body was found in Riverside County. She had been strangled.

The couple's next target was 35-year-old Pamela Simmons, who disappeared on 28 October in Bullhead City. She too had been abducted while withdrawing money from a cash machine and her vehicle was also found abandoned nearby. A third girl was kidnapped and killed just ten days later in Redlands. Twenty-year-old Corinna Novis had been taken from a shopping mall in broad daylight.

The fourth person to be murdered was 19-year-old psychology student Lynel Murray. Her boyfriend reported her missing on 12 November after she had missed a date. He found her car parked outside the dry-cleaning shop in Orange County where she worked and contacted the police. The following day her body was discovered in a Huntington Beach motel room. She was naked and there was evidence of sexual assault. At this point the police were sure they were looking for a serial killer because an almost identical method had been employed in each of the four slayings, but they had no inkling that a woman was involved or that the crimes had been committed by a couple.

But then they got lucky.

The Killers Left Their Names Behind

A chequebook belonging to Corinna Novis was found in a dumpster at Laguna Niguel. It was stuffed into a fast food bag that also contained a bill with the names of the customers on it – Cynthia and James Marlow. The same day the police were called to a San Bernardino motel where the couple had stayed. They had passed the time practising Lynel Murray's signature on motel stationery and left this evidence behind them. A nationwide search was initiated, which led to a tip-off from the owner of a mountain lodge at Big Bear City, California. A huge police contingent surrounded the lodge but the occupants had fled. They were spotted a few hours later on a mountain pass, where they were apprehended without a struggle.

Whatever alibis they might have rehearsed fell apart when the police pointed out to them that they were both wearing clothes known to have been stolen from the dry cleaners where victim Lynel Murray had worked.

Cynthia confessed and then offered to show the detectives where they had buried the body of Corinna Novis, who had been sodomized and strangled. The forensic evidence against the couple was compelling. Their fingerprints were recovered from Corinna's car and Cynthia was identified by the owner of the pawnshop where she had sold the dead woman's typewriter.

On 17 November 1986 the pair were formally charged with the murders. As the date for the trial approached the recriminations began. By the time they took the stand their enmity was raw, each blaming the

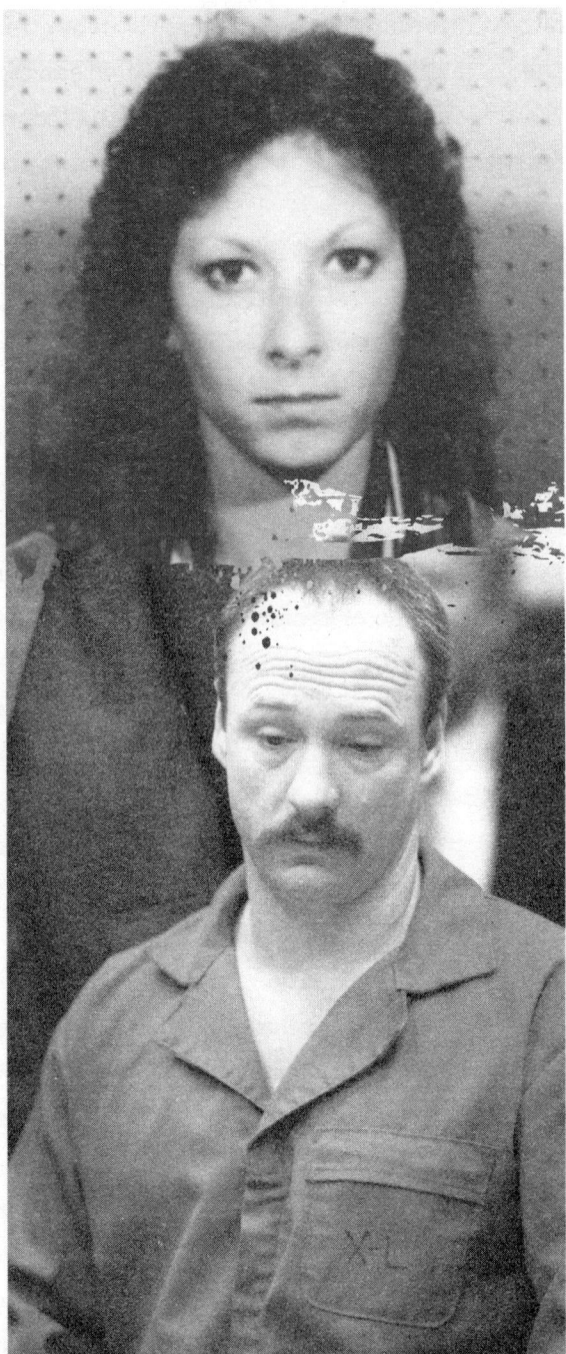

Coffman left her life of privilege and ended up with Marlow.

other for their fate. When she was asked if she needed anything, Cynthia told her lawyer that all she wanted was some way of erasing the tattoo from her buttocks. Then on 30 August 1989 a guilty verdict was returned for both parties on all counts and the sentence of death was recorded.

An appeal for a retrial was made to the California Supreme Court, on the grounds that the couple should have been tried separately, but in August 2004 the petition was rejected. Justice Kathryn M. Werdegar concluded that there was sufficient independent evidence against both defendants and that an abuse of discretion had not denied them separate trials. The case against them was so strong that any error in not ordering a separate trial would have been 'harmless beyond a reasonable doubt'.

Justice Werdegar rejected Cynthia's claim that she had only acted as an accomplice because Marlow had beaten her and threatened to harm her six-year-old son and she dismissed Marlow's attempts to blame Cynthia for the California killings. Marlow had testified that it had been Cynthia's idea to kill Corinna Novis, whereas he had only intended to rob her, but witnesses – including Coffman's cellmate – had confirmed that each of the accused had taken credit for the murder.

The judge also rebuffed Coffman's contention that she should not be executed because she was less culpable than Marlow.

'... Coffman, 24 years old at the time of the offenses, was found by the jury to have committed murder and to have engaged in the charged felonies with the intent to kill or to aid or abet Marlow in killing the victim. The jury also heard evidence that Coffman, together with Marlow, had committed another similar murder and other felony offenses in Orange County. Evidently the jury was not persuaded that Coffman suffered from such physical abuse or emotional or psychological oppression as to warrant a sentence less than death. Contrary to Coffman's argument, the offenses here were of the most serious nature, and her sentence clearly befits her personal culpability.'

RAY AND FAYE COPELAND

Murderers invariably have a motive. Some kill in cold blood for profit, or for sexual or sadistic satisfaction. Others kill in the heat of passion – they might be avenging an imagined insult or trying to prevent a former lover from leaving them. Many commit murder to conceal a crime. A few might even believe that they are carrying out a mercy killing to end the suffering of another, or that they have been chosen by a vengeful God to kill in his name.

Nebraska couple Ray and Faye Copeland might have been unique in that they murdered complete strangers because they simply could not think of another way of life. Ray is thought to have murdered as many as 12 vagrants and runaways during the 1970s and 1980s, after they had served their purpose in his fraudulent livestock deals, while his wife Faye kept silent. A dull, callous man, he saw the men's deaths as akin to killing a stray dog. He took no particular pleasure in it but he did not give it a second thought either, while his wife maintained that it was not her business to criticize her husband.

'I was raised to love my husband and support him no matter what,' she later said. 'The man is the head of the family. The Bible says it should be that way... Maybe we'd have got along better if I had knocked the sh*t out of him a few times.'

In August 1989 a 57-year-old farm labourer named Jack McCormick contacted the Nebraska police with an incredible story about a farmer who had tried to kill him back in Missouri. It was after McCormick had stumbled upon the farmer's scheme to buy livestock with worthless cheques signed by drifters and vagrants like himself. But that was not all. Before he ran for his life, McCormick had unearthed human bones on his employer's land, which made him suspect that other farm workers might not have been as lucky as he had been.

The Missouri authorities might have dismissed the claims as the mischievous act of a disgruntled employee had it not been for the fact that the farmer had been under suspicion for some time.

Copeland, 76 years old at the time, had a thick file for theft and fraud going back a long way, but he had evaded arrest by pointing to the fact that the signatures on the worthless cheques were not his. He had been seen in the company of the murdered drifters on the day of the cattle market and had been giving them the nod as to what and when to buy, but the men could not be traced when the cheques they had signed were returned unpaid by the bank.

The local sheriff decided that he needed to unearth the evidence before Copeland could destroy it. So early on the morning of 9 October 1989, Sheriff Leland O'Dell arrived on Copeland's land with 40 officers and dozens of bloodhounds. They began searching the property.

The Grisly Quilt

The investigators spent a fruitless week scouring the acres of farmland but eventually their thoroughness paid off. Three bodies were found in shallow graves in a barn that stood on an adjacent plot. All three were young males who had been shot once in the back of the head. They were later identified as Paul Cowart, from Arkansas, John Freeman, from Oklahoma, and Jimmie Harvey, from Missouri.

A fourth body, that of Wayne Warner, was found wrapped in plastic sheeting under the floor of a barn at another location and a fifth was discovered nearby. It was that of Dennis Murphy.

The last two men had also been killed by a bullet in the back of the head. Ballistic tests subsequently identified Ray Copeland's .22 calibre rifle as the murder weapon. Copeland's wife Faye was also indicted because detectives had found a list of 12 names in her handwriting, all with an 'X' by the side. All of the named men were missing persons and five of them were linked with the bodies found at the farm. It was later discovered that Faye Copeland had used material from the men's clothing to make a quilt.

The police were anxious to trace the other missing men so they offered Faye a deal, but she refused to co-operate, insisting that she had no knowledge of the killings. At her trial in November 1990 she claimed that she had not attempted to stop her husband's homicidal activities because she was a battered wife and in fear of her life. But the incriminating list she had made, together with the quilt, convinced the jury that she was an accomplice to first degree murder. The judge sentenced her to death by lethal injection. When Ray was asked by the sheriff for his reaction his muttered response was terse.

'Well, those things happen to some, you know.'

Ray Copeland's trial began six months later, following a thorough assessment of his mental health. With no grounds to support an insanity plea his defence was hopeless and he was convicted on all counts and sentenced to death. Two years later the 78-year-old suffered a fatal heart attack while he awaited execution, so he took the location of the other victims to the grave with him.

On 6 August 1999 the death sentence imposed upon 78-year-old Faye Copeland was commuted to life imprisonment. Three years later she had a stroke and was permitted to leave the prison for a nursing home where she died in December 2003 aged 82. At one of the later hearings for clemency she restated her innocence.

'God will forgive me for anything I've said or done.'

AGNES AND ANDRÁS PÁNDY

ousey, middle-aged Agnes Pándy stared blankly from behind her prescription spectacles at the detective who had just entered the interview room at Brussels police headquarters. As he sat down and pulled out a pen to make his preliminary notes, he must have wondered what information the dowdy librarian might have that could be of use to him. When she spoke it was in a voice as expressionless as her face: 'I am my father's sex slave.'

Graphic Detail

She then described in graphic detail the bullying and abuse she claimed she had been subjected to from the age of 13. But that was not all. That spring afternoon in 1992 she also accused her father of murdering her stepmother Edit Fintor and her stepsister Andrea four years earlier. Agnes and her older brother had been sent away to the coast and when they returned her father had a message for them. 'Don't look for them. They're not coming back.'

Frustrated Spinster

The detective was not inclined to believe her incredible story. For one thing her father was a respectable Protestant pastor in Molenbeek, an impoverished district in the Belgian capital. And besides, the 'victim' was thought to be alive and well and living in Eastern Europe. In a lengthy interview later that day Pastor Pandy vigorously dismissed his daughter's accusations as the fantasies of a frustrated spinster who had been pathologically jealous of her stepmother. He suggested that the impressionable Agnes had been brainwashed by a religious sect who implanted false memories in their members to alienate them from their families. As for the lurid accusations of murder, Pandy was able to produce letters purporting to be from his estranged second wife, which appeared to substantiate his story that she had returned to Hungary with her daughter, some years earlier. Subsequent enquiries revealed that he had registered her as 'missing' at the time of her disappearance in 1987. Fortunately for him the investigating officer was traced and when questioned he recalled how distraught Pandy had seemed at the time. If the pastor had been putting on an act, it had been a very convincing performance.

The Dutroux Factor

The police were inclined to dismiss the abuse as a story told by a neurotic girl desperate for attention, so the report was stamped 'case closed', filed away and forgotten. Forgotten, that is, until 1997 when the file was reopened in response to the public outcry surrounding an unrelated case, that of child killer Marc Dutroux. It had been rumoured that prominent members of the Belgian establishment might have conspired to cover up Dutroux's crimes in order to divert attention from their alleged involvement in a paedophile ring. So in a desperate effort to refute the rumours and restore public confidence in the judicial system the Belgian authorities ordered all cold case files to be reopened and all unproven accusations over the past decade to be re-examined. It was an instinctive response to quieten public anger and it was not expected to

Family affair: Agnes claimed that incest had led her father to murder, but no one believed what she was saying to them.

produce any results. But in such trying times even the word of a pastor could be questioned.

Agnes was recalled to police headquarters, where she was closely questioned. In the wake of the Dutroux scandal she had been making accusations in the Belgian press, which had forced the authorities to look more closely at her original statement.

'I am ashamed that my father might turn out to be one of the worst serial killers in history,' she had told a reporter.

Such serious allegations demanded thorough and immediate investigation.

Dissolving the Bodies

This time she was interviewed by senior prosecutor François Monsieur who took her story more seriously. Sensing that she was finally being listened to, Agnes opened up and spoke for a total of seven hours over a two-day period. Her story shocked even the hardened prosecutor, who struggled to maintain an appearance of professional detachment while she recalled the clinical means by which she and her father had butchered six members of their own family and disposed of the remains. Between 1986 and 1992 they had killed Ilona Sores, Edit Fintor and her daughters Tunde and Andrea as well as Agnes' two younger brothers, Zoltan and Daniel.

'It was my task to take out the organs while he [Pandy] was cutting up the remains,' she confessed as if describing a routine household chore. 'I just used a kitchen knife... you have to exercise strength. It's not that easy.'

She had eviscerated one of her own stepsisters while her father had chopped up the corpse with an axe. When asked to describe how she had felt the only word she could summon was 'cold'. Agnes claimed that they had dismembered the victims and then dumped bags of bloody flesh at the local abattoir, hoping that no one would notice the difference between human remains and horsemeat. But there was too much evidence to dispose of in that way and besides, the heads and the limbs would have to be destroyed. These were dropped into a bath of household cleaning fluid and chemically dissolved until nothing identifiable remained but human soup, which could be flushed down the drain.

When the case came to court, prosecutors feared that the jury might look at the two unprepossessing individuals in the dock and find it impossible to believe that they could have dismembered and disposed of so many corpses. And so they devised a demonstration in which forensic scientists dissolved body parts in a vat of the household cleaning fluid. The remains had been harvested from a man who had died of natural causes and had donated his body to science. As Agnes had predicted the flesh simply melted from the bones. The experiment was filmed and the footage was shown in court. Pandy watched the video impassively. Agnes turned away.

Pandy was sentenced to life imprisonment on six counts of murder. Agnes got 21 years.

GWENDOLYN GRAHAM AND CATHERINE WOOD

It is a sad and sobering fact that not all nurses and doctors are caring and compassionate professionals who put the wellbeing of their patients first. Michigan nurses Gwendolyn Gail Graham, 23, and Catherine May Wood, 24, might have been qualified to care for the elderly but they were certainly not compassionate or caring by nature. Quite the opposite, in fact.

The two women first met at the Alpine Manor Nursing Home in Walker, Michigan in 1987 where Wood was employed as a head nurse and Graham as her assistant. They became lesbian lovers and practised asphyxia to heighten their sexual pleasure. One thing led to another and before long they were discussing strangling their patients for kicks, going so far as to choose victims whose initials would spell out M-U-R-D-E-R, just in case the police were too slow to catch on. But the elderly women Graham chose for her first victims put up such a struggle that she had to give up. Incredibly, none of her intended victims alerted the other staff or accused Graham of assault.

Graham then chose a victim who would not fight back. She was a patient with Alzheimer's disease who was smothered to death with little effort, while Wood kept a lookout. The next victims were easy to dispatch too. Wood stood guard outside their rooms, while Graham

Gwen Graham (top) and Cathy Wood were lovers who got their kicks by taking the lives of helpless victims.

suffocated them with a washcloth. Money was not the prime motive, even though the helpless women were robbed of their jewellery – the pair were sexually aroused by killing. They frequently slipped into an empty bedroom to satiate their lust as they relived the grisly details.

181

While they were there they fingered the souvenirs they had stolen from the crime scene. They did not just take jewellery and other valuables. Often it was mundane items, such as the victim's dentures. More appalling was the revelation that they even experienced sexual stimulation while preparing the bodies in the mortuary.

Yet no one employed at the nursing home suspected that the pair were acting oddly. Even when they boasted of what they were doing, their confessions were dismissed as a sick joke.

All the while Wood had been the passive partner, acting as lookout while Graham did the grisly deed, but then Graham demanded that Wood take a turn. She refused, transferring to another shift to avoid being taunted by her now former lover. Graham, however, was insatiable. She found another lesbian partner and then took a job in a hospital maternity unit in Texas. Wood broke down and confessed all to her ex-husband when she heard that Graham had threatened to kill one of the babies, but he would not believe her.

He refused to go to the police. It was not until a year later that he finally relented, at which point the terrible truth came to light.

Graham and Wood played their so-called 'murder game' for about three months, during which time it is thought that they murdered as many as 40 elderly patients, though they were initially charged with killing five. Wood bargained for a lenient sentence by turning state's evidence, laying all the blame on her dominant, sadistic former partner. Graham's defence counsel countered that Wood had invented the whole story in order to avenge herself on Graham for taking a new lover, but the jury was not buying it. Graham was convicted of first degree murder in all five cases and one count of conspiracy to commit murder, for which she received six concurrent life sentences, with no possibility of parole.

PAUL BERNARDO AND KARLA HOMOLKA

On the surface, Paul Bernardo and Karla Homolka seemed the most unlikely of serial killers. They were a middle-class young Canadian couple, both good-looking and fair-haired. However, these ostensibly model citizens conspired together in the rape, torture and murder of at least three young women, including Karla's own sister, Tammy. At her trial, Karla blamed all the crimes on her abusive husband Paul. Subsequent evidence showed that she herself was just as deeply implicated. However, it is probably true to say that without Bernardo, Homolka would never have killed – while Bernardo almost certainly would have done, whether or not he had had a lover to aid and abet him.

Abusive Father

Paul Bernardo was born in the well-to-do Toronto suburb of Scarborough in August 1964, the third child of accountant Kenneth Bernardo and home-maker Marilyn. At least that is what Paul believed when he was growing up; it was only when he was 16 that his mother revealed him to be the offspring of an affair she had had. By this time, it was abundantly clear that all was not well in the seemingly respectable Bernardo household. Kenneth was physically abusive to his wife and sexually abusive to his daughter; meanwhile, Marilyn had become grossly overweight and remained virtually housebound.

Nevertheless, up to that point Paul appeared to be a happy, well-adjusted child, who enjoyed his involvement in scouting activities. It was only when he became a young man that he revealed a darker side to his nature. He was attractive, charming and, not surprisingly, popular with women. However, his sexual appetites turned out to be anything but charming. He would beat up the women he went out with, tie them up and force them to have anal sex. This behaviour carried on through his time at the University of Toronto, a period during which he also developed a money-making sideline in smuggling cigarettes into the US. After leaving college, he got a job as an accountant at Price Waterhouse. Not long afterwards, in October 1987, he met Karla Homolka.

Karla Homolka was born on 4 May 1970 in Port Credit, Ontario, the daughter of Dorothy and Karel Homolka. She had two sisters, Lori and Tammy. Like Bernardo's, this was a middle-class family, but in this case it seemed to be a genuinely happy one. Karla was a popular girl who attended Sir Winston Churchill High School and then became a veterinary assistant, working at an animal hospital, which was where she met Paul Bernardo.

Unlike most of his previous girlfriends, Karla was not repulsed by her new boyfriend's sexual sadism. Instead, she joined in enthusiastically, encouraging him to go ever further into his dark fantasies. Before long, this meant going out and finding women to rape. Over the next few years, Bernardo carried out well over a dozen rapes around the Scarborough area. How far Homolka was involved is not entirely clear, though one victim reported seeing a woman lurking behind the rapist, filming the event.

The police took a long time to deal with the case. In 1990, they finally released a photo-fit sketch that produced an immediate identification of Paul Bernardo. A blood test was taken from Bernardo, revealing that he had the same blood group as the rapist. Further tests were called for. Unbelievably, it took the police laboratory three years to carry out detailed tests, which proved conclusively that Bernardo was the 'Scarborough Rapist'. By that time, however, he was also a murderer.

As time went on, raping strangers was no longer enough for Bernardo. He developed a fantasy about raping Karla's 15-year-old sister Tammy. Once again, Karla was a willing accomplice. She decided to drug Tammy, using anaesthetic stolen from the veterinary clinic where she worked. On 24 December 1990, Karla got Tammy drunk and administered a drug called Halothane to her. Both Paul and Karla then raped Tammy and videotaped the entire episode. They did not initially intend to kill Tammy but the anaesthetic caused her to choke on her own vomit, and she died on her way to hospital. The official cause of death was suffocation. Karla's grieving parents put the tragedy down to an accident, caused by Tammy having drunk too much.

Marriage of Minds

Karla grieved briefly but was soon engrossed in planning her wedding that summer. A few weeks beforehand, she lured one of her friends, a teenager named Jane, round to the house and gave her the same treatment she had doled out to her sister. This time, though, Jane survived the experience, awaking from her drugged sleep confused and sore, but unaware that she had been raped by both Karla and Paul. This lapse of memory undoubtedly saved her life.

The couple's next victim, 14-year-old Leslie Mahaffy, was not so lucky. Paul abducted her on 15 July 1991 and the couple raped and tortured the girl over a 24-hour period, filming the event, before Paul finally killed her. Her body was found soon afterwards, dismembered and encased in cement on Lake Gibson. The same day that Mahaffy's body was found, Paul and Karla were married in a lavish affair at Niagara.

Two of a kind: Karla could be heard encouraging Paul as she filmed him raping one of his victims.

Four months later, on 30 November 1991, 14-year-old Terri Anderson disappeared. She may well have been murdered by Bernardo and Homolka, but the case remains unproven. Their final victim was 17-year-old Kristen French, abducted from a church parking lot on 16 April 1992. This time, the couple kept their victim alive for three days, raping and torturing her. They finally murdered her when they realized they were due to attend an Easter dinner at Karla's parents' house.

This was the last murder the couple committed. By the summer of 1992, Bernardo had started to take out his rage on Homolka and in

January 1993 she left him. The following month, the police lab finally ran the test on Bernardo's blood sample and discovered that he was the Scarborough Rapist. As Bernardo's name had also come up in the investigations into the murders of Mahaffy and French, the police finally put the whole case together. Homolka successfully painted herself as just another victim of the dominating Bernardo, and agreed a plea bargain whereby she would plead guilty to manslaughter and receive a 12-year prison sentence in return for testifying against Bernardo.

Willing Partner

Homolka's trial duly began in June 1993. She once again played the abused wife and received the agreed sentence. However, two years later, when Bernardo's trial began and the prosecution revealed the new evidence of Bernardo's videotapes, the judge and jury were able to see, in all too graphic detail, how willing a partner Homolka had been in the rape and torture of Mahaffy and French. Bernardo did his best to put the blame back on to Homolka, but the videotapes were utterly damning, and he received a life sentence in prison. As a result of her deal with prosecutors, Homolka was released from prison in 2005 and reported to be living with her new husband and three children in Montreal in 2011.

DAVID PARKER RAY AND CINDY HENDY

Truth or Consequences, New Mexico was once a place of relaxation. The first people to enjoy its hospitality arrived over one hundred years ago. They were there to soak in the Geronimo Springs at John Cross Ranch. It would be the first of several dozen spas to be built around the heated groundwater that continues to bubble up in this city of less than 8,000 souls. The entire community was built around this natural phenomenon. Anyone who wonders how important it once was to the local economy need look no further than the city's original name: Hot Springs. The city became Truth or Consequences in 1950, when the popular radio quiz show of that name offered to broadcast from the first community to rename itself after the show. It was all good fun.

The first indication of David Parker Ray's crimes came on 26 July 1996, when the sheriff's office in Truth or Consequences received a call from a young Marine. On the previous day he had argued with his wife Kelly Van Cleave and he had not seen or heard from her since. The anxious husband received only advice.

His wife had been gone such a short time that she could not be considered as a missing person. Based on past experience, the office had every reason to believe that Kelly would turn up.

Sure enough, the young man's wife returned home on the very next day. She had been brought back by an employee of nearby Elephant Butte State Park, where she had been found wandering in a dazed and incoherent state.

Kelly could account for only a few of the many hours she had been missing. After the fight with her husband, she remembered going to a friend's house. This was followed by trips to a number of bars, the last of which was the Blue Waters Saloon. It was there that Kelly ordered a beer, her first drink of the evening.

She soon began to feel dizzy. The sensation was not dissimilar to being drunk, but something was not quite right. Kelly could recall little else from this point onwards, though she was certain that an old friend, Jesse Ray, had offered to help. Those missing hours brought an end to Kelly's marriage. Her husband could never accept her disappearance, or her claim that she could not remember what had happened.

Nightmares

Jesse Ray might have been able to help... but she could not be found. Kelly soon left Truth or Consequences, never to return. She would never see Jesse again.

Now separated, Kelly began to suffer from nightmares. The horrifying images were remarkably consistent – she saw herself being tied to a table, being gagged with duct tape and having a knife held to her throat. Nothing quite made sense so Kelly never did report her strange experience to the authorities. All the sheriff's office at Truth or Consequences had on file was a seemingly trivial phone call from a distrusting husband. They could not have known that the woman who walked through their door on 7 July 1997 was bringing information that was related to Kelly's disappearance.

The woman had come to report that she had not heard from her 22-year-old daughter, Marie Parker, for several days. This time, there would be an investigation. In such a small city, it was not difficult to track the young woman's movements. Marie had last been seen on 5 July at the Blue Waters Saloon. She had been drinking with Jesse Ray. Jesse told the authorities that Marie had been drinking heavily so she had driven her home, but she had not seen her since.

But Jesse was not the only person that Marie had been drinking with on the night of her disappearance. Roy Yancy, an old boyfriend, had also been raising a glass at the Blue Waters Saloon. A Truth or Consequences boy born and raised, there was nothing in Roy's past to make the community proud.

As a child he had been part of a gang that had roamed Truth or Consequences strangling cats, poisoning dogs and tipping over gravestones, acts that led the city to cancel that year's Hallowe'en festivities. He had also received a dishonourable discharge from the navy.

Marie might well have been in the company of an unsavoury character, but the Truth or Consequences sheriff's office saw nothing unusual about her disappearance. After all, the city was known for its transient population. They were all too ready to accept someone's hazy recollection of a girl accepting a ride out of the city. It was a typical story.

At around this time a new woman arrived in the small city. Cindy Hendy's history was anything but enviable. A victim of sexual abuse, she had been molested by her stepfather before being turned out on the street at the age of 11. Cindy had been a teenage mother, but only in the sense that she had given birth – other people had taken on the job of raising her daughter. When she arrived in Truth or Consequences, Cindy was on the run from a drugs charge. Several months earlier, she had supplied cocaine to an undercover agent. She was a violent woman with a short fuse, so it was not long before she found herself in the local jail. Days later she was sent out to Elephant Butte Lake on a work-release programme. It was there that she first met David Parker Ray, the father of her friend Jesse.

He was a quiet, though approachable and friendly man. Ray had been a neglected child. Unloved by his mother, his only real contact with his drifter father came in the form of periodic drunken visits. These invariably ended with the old man leaving behind a bag of pornographic magazines that portrayed sadomasochistic acts. His adult life was one of many marriages and many jobs. He had lived a transient life before 1984, when he settled down with his fourth wife in Elephant Butte. After acquiring a run-down bungalow on a little piece of property, Ray supported them by working as an aircraft engine repairman.

By 1995, his wife had left him. The fourth Mrs Ray would be the final Mrs Ray, but she was not his last companion. In January 1999, Cindy Hendy moved into Ray's bungalow. It mattered little that he was two decades older because the 38-year-old had met her soulmate – someone who, like herself, was obsessed with sadomasochistic sex.

Lonely Newcomer

Cindy had been living with Ray for just one month when, on 16 February, she invited Angie Montano over for a visit. Angie, a single mother, was new to Truth or Consequences, and was eager to make friends. She had come to the wrong place, because she was blindfolded, strapped to a bed and sexually assaulted. Ray and Cindy's sadistic tastes went beyond rape. Angie was stunned by cattle prods and various other devices that Ray had made himself. After five days, Angie managed to get Ray to agree to her release. He drove her to the nearest highway and let her out. As luck would have it, she was picked up by a passing off-duty police officer. Angie shared her story with him, but she would not agree to making an official report. Just as Kelly Van Cleave had done four years earlier, Angie left Truth or Consequences, never to return.

Even as the assaults on Angie Montano were taking place, Cindy's mind was sometimes elsewhere. Though her 39th birthday had only just passed, she was about to become a grandmother. She made plans

Ray revelled in the power he held over helpless victims; Hendy was his willing accomplice.

to attend the birth in her old hometown of Monroe, Washington, but before she could go she needed to find a sex slave for Ray, someone who would meet his needs in her absence.

On 18 March, they drove through the streets of Albuquerque in Ray's motorhome, where they came upon Cynthia Vigil. She was a prostitute, so it was not difficult to get her into the vehicle, nor was it hard to overpower the 22-year-old. After being bound, Cynthia was taken back to the Elephant Butte bungalow, where she was collared, chained, blindfolded and gagged. A tape was then played to her. The voice was Ray's.

> 'Hello, bitch. Well, this tape's gettin' played again. Must mean I picked up another hooker. And I'll bet you wonder what the hell's goin' on here. The gag is necessary because after a while you're goin' to be doin' a lot of screaming.'

Those were just the first few sentences in a recording that lasted over five minutes. Ray went on to describe how he and his 'lady friend' were going to rape and torture the listener.

True to the words of the tape, Ray and Cindy tortured and raped the prostitute over the course of the next three days. The assaults had no effect on Ray's work habits. As the fourth day began, he donned his state park uniform and drove off. Cindy was charged with keeping their victim under control. But his lady friend wasn't quite up to the task. In fact, she was downright sloppy.

When Cindy left the room to prepare a lunch of tuna sandwiches, the young prostitute noticed that her abductor had left behind the keys to her chains. After releasing herself, she grabbed the phone and called the Sierra County Sheriff's Office. Before she could say a word, Cindy was back in the room, bottle in hand. She took a violent swing at the prostitute, cutting her with the breaking glass. Cynthia noticed an ice pick while she was lying on the floor. She quickly grabbed it and stabbed her captor in the back of the neck.

It was not a lethal blow, but it was enough to give Cynthia time to get out of the house. Naked except for a dog collar and chain, she ran out of the door and down the dusty, unpaved street. She was spotted by the drivers of two cars, but they just swerved to avoid the distressed, bleeding woman.

After about a mile, she came upon a trailer home. She burst through the door and fell at the feet of a woman watching television.

Scene of the Crime

Just minutes after the first interrupted call, the Sierra County Sheriff's Office received a second one. When the authorities arrived at the mobile home they heard a horrific tale of torture and assault. As Cynthia Vigil was being transported to the local hospital, the sheriff's department decided to call in the state police.

Over a dozen officers converged on Ray's bungalow, only to find that Cindy had fled.

The house was a mess, with garbage littering the floor. If there was any order, it was found in Ray's instruments of torture, which were arranged on hooks hanging from the walls of several rooms. His library included books featuring Satanism, torture and violent pornography. There were also a number of medical books, which presumably enabled him to carry out many of his fantasies.

The hunt was now on for Ray and Cindy. The chase was as short as it was easy. The couple had not fled – instead, they were driving along the nearby roads, looking for their captive. Ray and Cindy were spotted within 15 minutes, a mere two blocks from their home. They quickly admitted that they had been looking for Cynthia Vigil, but they also came up with an implausible explanation for their actions. The abduction of the prostitute had been a humanitarian act, claimed Ray and Cindy. Her confinement had been nothing more than an effort to help the young woman kick her addiction to heroin.

The story fooled no one. Ray and Cindy were arrested and taken into custody. As the investigation of Ray's property began, the state law enforcement officials realized that they did not have the resources to deal with their discoveries. Lieutenant Richard Libicer of the New Mexico State Police explained the situation:

'I think it's safe to say that nothing that was inside that house was anything any of us had experienced before – or come across before – except maybe in a movie somewhere. It was just completely out of the realm of our experience.'

The assortment of shackles and pulleys and other instruments of torture inside the bungalow appeared almost mundane compared to what was discovered inside a padlocked semi-trailer that was parked outside.

What Ray described as the 'Toy Box' contained hundreds of torture devices. Many of them, such a machine that was used to electrocute women's breasts, had been designed and built by the former mechanic. At the centre of this horror was a gynaecology table. Cameras were installed, so that the women could see what was happening to them. Ray had also videotaped his assaults, including the one involving Kelly Van Cleave. She had supposedly been found wandering by a state park official – but the state park official was David Parker Ray.

The videotapes were a revelation. For a start, they linked Jesse Ray to her father's crimes. Kelly's evidence also proved useful, but the most damning testimony came from Cindy Hendy.

Within days of her arrest, the 39-year-old turned on her boyfriend. She told the investigators that Ray had been abducting and torturing women for many years. What is more, Ray had told Cindy that his fantasies had often ended in murder.

Subsequent searches of Elephant Butte Lake and the surrounding countryside revealed nothing, but the police remained convinced that

Ray had killed at least one person. Cindy also confirmed that Jesse had participated in at least some of the abductions. She added that she often worked in tandem with Roy Yancy.

Soft Centre

Despite his tough demeanour, Roy caved in when he was arrested. He told the police that he and Jesse had drugged Marie Parker, the young woman who had gone missing three years earlier. They had taken her to Elephant Butte, where she was tortured. When Ray tired of her, he instructed Roy to kill the woman who had once been his girlfriend.

The body was never found.

Roy Yancy pleaded guilty to second degree murder and was sentenced to 20 years in prison.

After pleading guilty to kidnapping Kelly Van Cleave and Marie Parker, Jesse Ray received a nine-year sentence.

Facing the possibility of 197 years in prison, Cindy Hendy made a deal with the prosecutors. After pleading guilty to her crimes against

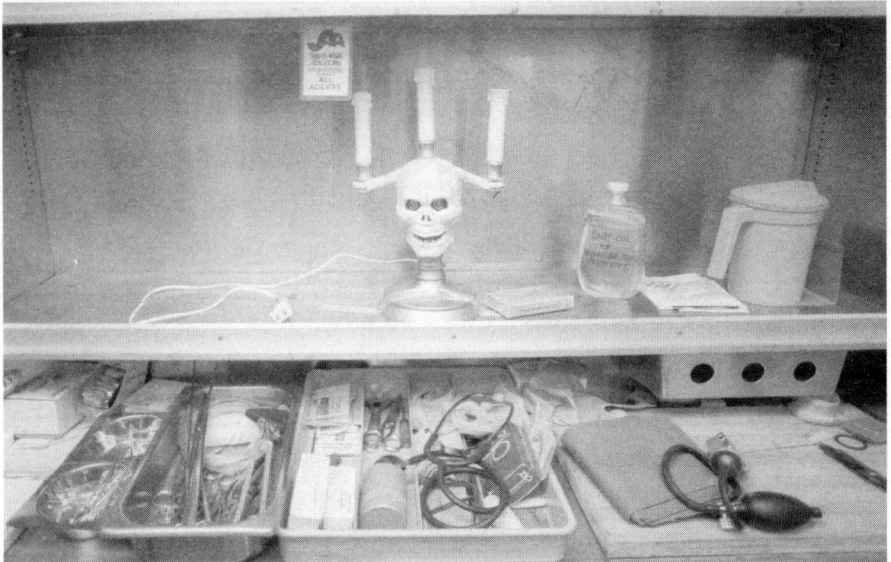

The 'Toy Box', a mobile torture chamber, was Ray's pride and joy – he put $100,000 into it.

Cynthia Vigil she received a 36-year sentence, with a further 18 years on probation.

Even Ray appeared to co-operate with the authorities, but only to the extent of describing his fantasies. He denied abducting or murdering anyone. Any sadomasochistic activities had been between consenting adults. 'I got pleasure out of the woman getting pleasure,' he told one investigator. 'I did what they wanted me to do.'

Ray faced three trials for his crimes against Kelly Van Cleave, Cynthia Vigil and Angie Montano. He was found guilty in the first trial, but part of the way through the second he too made a deal. Ray agreed to plead guilty in exchange for Jesse's release. The case concerning Angie Montano was never heard because she had died of cancer.

On 30 September 2001, David Parker Ray received a 224-year sentence for his crimes against Kelly Van Cleave and Cynthia Vigil. In the end, Ray did not serve so much as a year. On 28 May 2002 he slumped over in a holding cell, killed by a massive heart attack.

'Satan has a place for you. I hope you burn in hell forever,' Cynthia Vigil's grandmother had once yelled at him.

One wonders whether the words meant anything to Ray. The one sign he had put up in his 'Toy Box' read: 'SATAN'S DEN'.

JOHN BROWN AND SAMUEL COETZEE

South Africa has seen more than its fair share of bloodshed in its history, but the country that shook off the shackles of apartheid and reinvented itself as the 'rainbow nation' is not immune to the sordid reality that is murder.

Between 1993 and 1995 the country's newspaper headlines were dominated not by politics but by a series of violent murders and the frantic hunt for the perpetrators.

The first body was discovered on 30 August 1993, on a gravel road near Pretoria. On 3 November 1993 two more corpses were found near the town of Heidelberg – those of an unidentified 15-year-old boy and a 30-year-old man. Both had suffered bullet and stab wounds and both had ligature marks around the throat. Such injuries are indicative of 'overkill' – wounds which must have been inflicted by a person in a rage because they were far beyond what would have been needed to kill a person. No attempt had been made to cover the face in either case so the police were confident that the killer had no personal relationship with his victim before the fatal date.

Strangled and Mutilated

A fourth victim, who had been strangled and mutilated, was found at Krugersdorp on 1 September 1995. His genitals had been cut off, suggesting that the killer was likely to be either a woman or a homosexual male. But because the other victims were all too strongly built to have been subdued by a female, detectives worked on the assumption that the murderer was a homosexual male.

Gay clubs throughout the region were visited and the owners and customers were shown photographs of the victims. Several witnesses remembered seeing the dead men in the company of a known cross-dresser called 'Kim'. Inquiries revealed that his real name was Samuel Coetzee, then aged 26. But before he could be questioned a fifth body took detectives to a house in Constantia Court, Edenvale. Inquiries confirmed that this victim had also been seen leaving a nightclub with Coetzee. When he was arrested Coetzee blamed his lover John Brown for the killings and claimed that he had only disposed of the bodies.

When 32-year-old Brown was brought in he attempted to put the blame on Coetzee. His only interest had been to rob the men. It was Coetzee, he said, who murdered them in a frenzied attack.

Before the truth could be drawn out of them Coetzee took an overdose of pills in his cell and died, leaving a suicide note saying he no longer wanted to go on living. In 1997, Brown was sentenced to life imprisonment and the following day the newspapers returned to the more immediate concerns of politics, scandal and sport.

BRYAN AND DAVID FREEMAN

Brothers Bryan and David Freeman may have been cut from the same cloth, but they bore no similarity to their parents. There were others like them, however, including their cousin Benny Birdwell. The trio were so often found together that they were often referred to as 'the Three Musketeers'. Desite the nickname, they had nothing in common with the heroes, Athos, Porthos and Aramis. And the setting of Alexandre Dumas' novel, 17th-century France, would not have suited them. No, the three boys would have felt most at home during the darkest, most violent days of Nazi Germany.

The Freeman boys weren't German, nor were they of German descent. They had never been to Germany; indeed these boys from Allentown, Pennsylvania had never been outside the United States.

Bryan and David's father, Dennis, was a high school custodian and Brenda, their mother, was a housewife. Devout Jehovah's Witnesses, they were a modest couple who never wanted to draw attention to themselves. But life was bleak in the Freeman home in Allentown, particularly for a child, because Dennis and Brenda dedicated themselves to raising their children in accordance with the dictates of the Governing Body of Jehovah's Witnesses. Each December, Bryan and David looked on with envy as other children played with their new toys – Christmas was not celebrated in the Freeman household. Nor were birthdays. The two boys were not allowed to attend birthday parties and they could not look forward to their own. As he grew into adolescence, Bryan came to resent the fact that he had been deprived of many of the activities that were enjoyed by others of his age.

In 1991, Bryan and David left the church. That they did so together was not surprising. They were close allies in an increasingly hate-filled rebellion against their parents and everything they stood for. Bryan was 13 years old at the time and David was two years younger, yet their physical stature was that of much older boys. They were more than capable of carrying out the threats of violence they had made against their parents. Seven-year-old Erik, the third and final Freeman child, was also a target, for no other reason than the fact that he would not join his siblings in rejecting the church.

Forbidden Fruit

Dennis and Brenda's constant attempts to bring their two eldest sons back as Jehovah's Witnesses only heightened their resentment. The brothers embraced all things that had been forbidden. Born into a religion that condemned alcohol, the boys began to drink heavily. By the time they reached their mid-teens, Bryan and David began taunting their parents with talk of joining the military, a career path that went against the dictates of the church.

However, the military would never have considered the Freeman boys. It was nothing to do with their intelligence because Bryan had once been an honours student, and they were both fine physical specimens, standing over 6 ft (1.83 m) tall and weighing over 200 lb (90 kg). What would have prevented their admission into the army were the tattoos on their foreheads. 'SIEG HEIL' read David's, while his brother's said 'BERZERKER'. Bryan also had a swastika tattooed on the right side of his neck. The tattoos advertised the fact that both brothers were proud white supremacists. Bryan had been introduced to the movement in 1992, during a stay at a substance abuse treatment facility. David always followed Bryan in whatever he did, so he had been an eager convert to the cause.

Together with their older cousin, Benny Birdwell, they formed their own small group of skinheads which they named 'Berzerker' after the 9th-century Norse warriors of that name. They replaced the religion of their parents with the racist religious ideology of Christian Identity and they began attending services preached by Mark Thomas on a farm not far from Allentown.

By 1995 the situation in the Freeman household was deteriorating and the threats of violence were escalating, so the desperate Freeman parents were looking for help and support outside their church. Brenda turned to a group for parents of troubled children, the Pennsylvania Human Relations Commission and the B'Nai Brith's Anti-Defamation League. In early February 1995, Dennis and Brenda went through their sons' bedrooms and threw out all of the neo-Nazi books, pamphlets, posters and clothing.

But the purge only resulted in more threats of violence and death. In fact, David began to speak quite openly about how he was going to kill his mother. And the killing would not stop there, he said. He would steal a gun, kill a policeman who had once crossed him and then head south to Florida. His words were dismissed as crazy by some who heard them, while others took them seriously – but they were too frightened to speak up. Bryan also seemed to be getting angrier at the world. On 23 February, the former honours student threatened the high school principal and was suspended for five days. He would never return to school.

Dennis and Brenda might not have recognized the imminent danger posed by their eldest sons, but young Erik was more perceptive. When his aunt, Valerie Freeman, asked him how he was getting along with his brothers, he was quick to respond.

'You never know when you're going to die,' he said.

He then asked her to take care of his dog because he was afraid that his brothers would kill it.

If anything, Bryan and David had come to hate their younger brother even more than their parents because he would not rebel.

Instead, the now 11-year-old boy was following a clearly defined path as a committed Jehovah's Witness.

Eerie Silence

On the afternoon of 27 February 1995, Valerie arrived at the Freemans' home to find Dennis' truck in the driveway. It was a strange sight – he had never been known to leave work early. Things became more surreal when she tried the front door and found it locked. Dennis and Brenda were so trusting that they never barred their doors. She eventually gained access through the sliding glass doors at the side of the house. Inside there was an eerie silence. She called out but there was no response, so she walked farther into the house, heading towards the bedrooms. Thoroughly unnerved by this time, Valerie stopped outside Erik's closed door and knocked. Still no response. When she opened the door, Valerie saw the boy lying in the middle of a bed that was soaked in blood. He was obviously dead. Panicking, she rushed down the hall to the master bedroom, where she found Dennis bludgeoned to death on the bed. His throat had been slashed and his face had been struck with such force that his brain was exposed.

Valerie fled from the house in horror. Running to a neighbour, she phoned the police.

What the authorities found confirmed Valerie's fleeting visions. They also saw something that Valerie had missed – a bloodied aluminium baseball bat was leaning against a china cabinet in the dining room. Both Erik and Dennis were dead, but where was Brenda?

The police moved methodically through the house, ever aware that the killer or killers might still be present. After covering the ground floor, they turned their attention to the basement. And there they found their answer. Brenda lay dead on the cellar floor, with the hem of her nightgown around her waist. No search was needed to find the murder weapons. A knife lay next to her still body and there was a bloodied lead pipe on the stairs. It seemed that the killers had left a calling card – two swastikas had been drawn on the wall above Brenda's head. If that wasn't a big enough clue, Bryan and David were missing and so was the family car. As it turned out, Benny had also disappeared.

Capturing the three killers did not take much in the way of detective work. The brutal murders of Dennis, Brenda and Erik had hit the media. What is more, the boys' tattoos made it nearly impossible for them to blend in with the general population.

On the day after the murders were discovered, a truck driver reported that he had spotted the skinheads in Hubbard, Ohio, some 320 miles (520 km) west of Allentown. The three fugitives had spent the night at the Truck World Motor Inn. Though they had disappeared by the time the police arrived at the motel, they had left an important clue behind them. There was a record of a telephone call to the family farm of neo-Nazi Frank Hesse, which was situated just outside Michigan's Hope Township, about 110 miles (180 km) north-east of Grand Rapids.

Bryan, David and Benny were caught the day after the murder at the home of skinhead Frank Hesse. The neo-Nazi, who knew Bryan only because they had once met at a concert in Detroit, proved a welcoming host. But then, the boys didn't bother telling him that they were on the run after having committed three murders.

On 1 March, Hesse took Bryan, David and Benny ice fishing. As they returned to the farm they were surrounded by members of the FBI and a Michigan State Police SWAT team.

All of them were taken into custody, though Hesse was soon released when it became apparent that he had known nothing of the murders in Allentown.

When questioned, each boy offered a different account of the events that had surrounded the deaths of Dennis, Brenda and Erik.

David, the first to speak, related that he had gone out for fast food and a movie with Bryan and David on 26 February, the evening before the bodies were discovered. They had arrived home at 10.30 pm, half an hour before the curfew Brenda had imposed. She had been waiting up for them. Rather than face their mother, Bryan, David and their cousin had crawled in through a basement window.

Third Time Unlucky

Hearing the commotion, Brenda went downstairs and told her sons to go to bed. When they did not do so, she came down a second time and asked Benny to leave. He complied with her request, but then he crept back in through the basement window. Brenda went downstairs a third time, David said, but he was by then in his basement bedroom with Benny. He had heard Bryan and Brenda yelling at each other, but the noise had soon stopped.

David claimed that he had not witnessed his mother's murder. In fact, he did not know it had taken place until Bryan walked into his room. At that point Bryan told the other boys that they would be stabbed if they did not go upstairs and finish Dennis and Erik off. David admitted that he had killed his father and brother, but Benny had done nothing more than act as a witness to the slaughter. The 15-year-old rounded off his story by saying that he had dumped the knives he had used in the kitchen sink, placed the bat in the dining room, changed his clothes and left home for good.

Benny told a very different tale, though it began in much the same way. He spoke of fast food, a movie and Brenda's confrontation with her eldest son. In the middle of the yelling match, Bryan went into his basement bedroom and returned with a steak knife. He then grabbed his mother, put his hand over her mouth, and stabbed her in the back. Brenda collapsed on to the floor, but she managed to reach backwards and remove the knife. Bryan managed to wrestle it away from her and he stabbed her in the shoulder in the process. He then stuffed a pair of shorts into her mouth so that her screams would not alert Dennis and Erik.

Following Brenda's murder, Benny said that he had remained in the basement while the two brothers went on to kill Dennis and Erik. After Bryan and David had changed, all three of them got in the Freeman family car and began arguing about what to do. It was Bryan who suggested that they should hide out at Hesse's farm in Michigan. As they travelled west, the young killers considered returning to the house. Perhaps they could make the murders look like the result of a burglary that had gone wrong. That idea went out of the window when news reports about the killings started coming through.

Innocent Bystander?

Benny insisted that he had nothing to do with the murders of Dennis, Brenda and Erik, despite his presence at the scene. He had joined the others in their escape because Bryan had told him not to 'puss out'. Benny's mother, who had driven to Michigan to see her son, believed his story. It mattered not one bit that his 'BERZERKER' tattoo matched Bryan's. Benny was 'a good boy'. In an effort to clear Benny's name, she told his story to a reporter from the *Midland Daily News*. Her efforts did him no favours.

What Benny's mother did not know was that the three boys had previously agreed on a plan of action. Working under the erroneous assumption that they could not be tried as adults, Bryan and David had agreed to take responsibility for the murders. That way Benny, an 18-year-old adult, would be saved from facing a murder trial. But when they read Benny's account of the murder in the *Midland Daily News*, the

Freeman brothers felt betrayed. Their sense of injury was compounded by the news that under Pennsylvania law minors charged with homicide are eligible to be tried in an adult court.

Although Bryan had been steadfastly silent about the killings, he could not keep quiet any longer. Speaking for David as well as for himself, he said that the brothers would provide the authorities with a formal statement if their conditions were met – that is, that the prosecution would not seek the death penalty, the brothers would retain the right to a trial and they would be granted an interview with a journalist of their choosing.

The terms of the deal were accepted by prosecutor Robert Steinberg. On 6 March, the day on which their parents and their brother were buried, David and Bryan told the authorities what had really happened in the Freeman home.

David repeated the story he had told earlier, but with a significant difference. The 15-year-old maintained that he had not witnessed his mother's murder. After she had been killed he went upstairs with Benny, going first to where his father was sleeping. Benny struck the first blow, hitting Dennis in the face with a pickaxe handle. David then joined in the beating, using the aluminium baseball bat. Finally, Benny finished Dennis off by cutting his throat. By this point David could not take any more, so it was left to Benny to kill Erik.

Bloody Shirt

Bryan told a nearly identical story, but he provided further details of Brenda's murder. He had stabbed her, much as his cousin had described, but Benny had not told the whole story. Bryan's cousin had clubbed Brenda with the pickaxe handle.

Steinberg was not satisfied with the two latest stories. Believing that both Bryan and David were lying, he cancelled the deal. After months of legal manoeuvring, the prosecution found evidence that contradicted Benny's story. Dennis Freeman's blood had been discovered on Benny's shirt, which discredited Benny's claim that he had stayed in the basement while the brothers had committed the murders upstairs.

On 7 December 1995, Bryan stood in court and admitted that he had killed his mother, thereby avoiding the death penalty. He was given a life sentence. A week later, David received an identical sentence after admitting that he had killed Dennis.

Only Benny would go to trial. On the first day of his trial, 26 March 1996, the defence revealed its strategy. With an IQ of 78, Benny was a follower, not a leader. He had blood on his shirt because he had walked into the bedroom as Dennis was being murdered.

On 26 April a jury decided that Benny had participated in the murder of Dennis Freeman. He was found guilty of murder in the first degree and was sentenced to life imprisonment without the possibility of parole.

FROGGIE AND MICKIE

Much has been written on the subject of criminal profiling and numerous theories have been offered to account for the aberrant behaviour of serial killers, who have been afforded a perverse form of celebrity status by our media-centred society. Clues to their sadistic compulsions are sought in their childhood and traumatic events in their lives are eagerly identified as the 'stressors' that set them off on their killing sprees. But many people have suffered rejection in their relationships, or have experienced bullying at school or the trauma of divorce, and yet they have still managed to keep their regrets, resentments and other personal feelings in check. And, conversely, not all serial killers conform to the typical or standard profile.

James Anthony Daveggio, the Californian serial rapist and sex killer who converted his minivan into a mobile torture chamber, had not wet his bed, tortured animals or set fire to property. Nor had he suffered from a head injury, physical disfigurement or abuse as a child. According to the criteria of criminal psychology he was alternately an organized and a disorganized lust killer, which means that he planned some of his offences while other attacks were opportunistic. Moreover, a psychiatric report that was compiled following his arrest for the sexual assault of six women and the murder of two more concluded that he was clinically sane and fit to stand trial. It seems that Daveggio and his equally depraved female partner Michelle 'Mickie' Michaud were simply oversexed, sadistic degenerates who had no self-control and no empathy for those they chose to inflict their sick fantasies upon.

The Making of a Murderer

It is believed that Daveggio might have claimed his first victim in 1974 at the tender age of 14. At that time he was one of a number of teenage boys questioned about the disappearance of 13-year-old Cassie Riley, whose partially clothed body was found on an embankment. Among other things, detectives noted the imprints of a pair of size ten trainers. There was no evidence of rape, but the victim had been beaten and then drowned in the creek. This suggested that her attacker had tried to force himself on her but when he had failed to perform he had lashed out and killed her. Witnesses reported seeing her talking with an older boy, who was wearing a green shirt with a patch on the sleeve. Daveggio was one of several boys interviewed, but another boy was eventually accused of the crime. However, Daveggio's sister later claimed that her mother had lied about his whereabouts to give him an alibi. Whatever the truth, he was then forgotten. Had he been formally questioned it might have put the brakes on his descent into even more serious crime.

Daveggio was brought up by his mother after his parents divorced. Without a father to set him straight he drifted into petty crime, stealing cars and fighting. Tired of hauling him out of trouble, his mother sent him to live with his father in Pacifica, California but that did not work out. Jim's hard-drinking dad was no role model so the boy was sent back to his mother. He continued to reoffend. His activities escalated to robbery, which earned him his first spell in the Alameda County boys' detention camp – where he picked up the nickname 'Froggie', together with a lifelong addiction to gambling and popping pills. On his release he proved to be a poster boy for the three-strikes-and-you're-out campaign by continually forcing himself on young girls, whom he had plied with liquor so that they could not cry rape. Although none of his predatory sexual assaults landed him in court, they were sufficiently serious to require him to submit to a psychiatric evaluation. It was decided that he was a sex offender who required treatment at the California Medical Facility in Vacaville. It was a short vacation for Daveggio, who celebrated his release by propositioning a female officer posing as a prostitute. He was driving under the influence of alcohol at the time.

With such a bulging young offender's record, Daveggio thought it might be wise to drop below the radar by moving to Sacramento, where in 1997 he joined a motorcycle gang known as the 'Devil's Horsemen'. The only problem was that he did not own a motorbike – but he knew someone who did, so he stole his. Then he dyed his hair and had his arms tattooed. With his new image, and a Harley-Davidson to impress the gang and their girls, he prowled the neighbourhood until he picked up prostitute Michelle 'Mickie' Michaud, who shared his sadomasochistic fantasies.

Sinister Role Model

He moved in with her and played 'daddy' to her daughters, but he had other games in mind. At first he enjoyed humiliating Mickie by complaining about whatever she did and treating her like a whore. Then he began bringing other women home and beating her when she protested. After being fired from his job as a barman, on suspicion of having robbed the safe, he turned to drug dealing. He sold crack cocaine from the house, which brought him to the attention of the police. When they discovered that he was a registered sex offender who was living in a house where there were children, they ordered him to move out. Even the motorcycle gang disowned him. It was at this point that he became obsessed with serial killers and decided that he wanted a share of their notoriety and 'the thrill of the kill'.

He modelled himself on killer Gerald Gallego, who had convinced his partner Charlene to procure a victim for him to molest and murder. Gallego felt that young girls would be wary of being approached by a

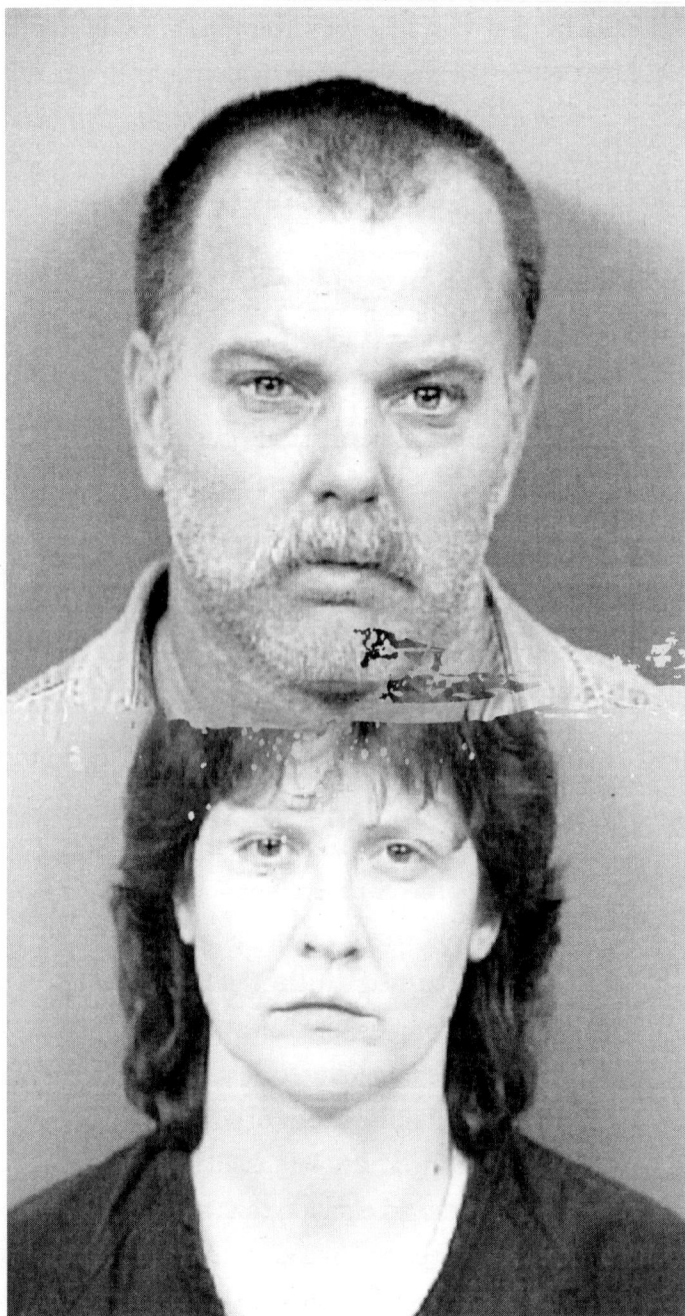

'Froggie' drifted into petty crime at a young age; 'Mickie' was a
prostitute who shared his sadomasochistic fantasies.

man, but he knew they could be persuaded to go with a woman, even if she was a stranger to them. Inspired by Gallego's example, Daveggio told Mickie to entice one of his daughter's friends to his house, where he would rape her. Once Mickie had proved herself to be a willing accomplice the pair set out on a hunt for victims. Twenty-year-old student Alicia Paredes was the first to be snatched off the street as she was walking home one evening. She was bundled into the van and driven to a remote location where she was raped – but she was allowed to live. It suited the couple's perverted power game to show mercy when it suited them. In this instance it was a fatal mistake because Alicia was able to tell the police that she remembered the man calling his female accomplice 'Mickie'. This detail was added to their file, together with a police artist's sketch of the couple drawn to match Alicia's description.

But it was not enough to save other girls from a similar fate. The next victim was forced to perform oral sex on 'Daddy' Daveggio, while Mickie held her down. A surfeit of booze and pills was making Daveggio lose his grip on reality, because he tried to comfort the girl after her ordeal and even sent Mickie to buy ice to soothe her injuries. He clearly had no grasp of the trauma he had subjected her to and must have imagined that he only had to console her to make everything all right again. He had depersonalized her, but in his self-centred world she was merely an object to gratify his desires and her pain was an inconvenience comparable with the needs of a demanding pet dog.

The pair's depravity reached a new low with their sexual assault on Mickie's daughter a few days later. Even her own offspring's pleading failed to move the psychotic woman, who held her down while Daveggio had oral sex with her. Some time later, still untroubled by their consciences, or even by the fear of being caught, the pair lured another female victim into the minivan with the promise of cocaine. Then they hit her over the head and demanded that she submit to degrading acts with Daveggio. But when the sobbing girl told them that the experience reminded her of what had happened with her stepfather, Daveggio lost interest. Mickie was not so easily turned off, however. She molested the girl and then took photographs, threatening to blackmail her if she went to the police.

The Torture Wagon

In early November Mickie was arrested for passing bad cheques, so she spent a short time in jail. While she was there Daveggio finished converting their vehicle. He kitted it out with ropes and chains to make his fantasy of a mobile torture wagon a reality.

As soon as Mickie was out the twosome resumed their 'adventures', but the next victim wriggled free and escaped. She was then able to give information to the police, which was backed up by statements from Daveggio's daughter and a friend of Mickie's daughter.

This put the police on the couple's trail, but they did not close in fast enough. Daveggio turned on his own daughter in a Sacramento motel. He raped her for a while and then Mickie joined in. When they were done he told his daughter that he wanted to torture her, but she threatened to scream for help so he promised to find someone else.

On the morning of 2 December Daveggio and Mickie were cruising around the California suburb of Pleasanton, eyeing up potential victims, when Daveggio picked 'the one with the pretty black hair'. He had chosen 22-year-old Vanessa Lei Samson, who was taking her regular walk to work. Two workmen on a nearby roof heard a piercing scream and the door of a van sliding shut. When they looked down they noticed a dark green minivan being driven by a woman. They assumed it was a mother and daughter arguing so they did not report it until the police asked for witnesses to the abduction.

Vanessa was gagged with a sex toy bought from a local store and then tortured with curling irons. When Daveggio had finished with her, he swapped places with Mickie and then drove to a hotel in South Lake

Tahoe, where they smuggled the girl into their room and subjected her to a prolonged and agonizing assault.

The last thing Vanessa ever heard was Daveggio's voice telling her that they were going to be 'bonded forever'.

As he said those words, he tightened a rope round her neck and strangled her. The couple dumped her body 30 ft (9 m) down an embankment in Alpine County and then returned to their motel, which was also in Tahoe.

Daveggio's Daughter Testifies

The next day, 3 December 1997, Mickie was due in court on the bad cheque charge but she did not turn up, so the police called at her home and talked her mother into revealing her whereabouts. They took the couple into custody without a struggle, but at this time they had no idea that the pair had committed anything more serious than fraud. However, Mickie had boasted about her role in Vanessa Lei Samson's murder to her cellmate, who reported the incident to detectives. It was then that they looked more closely at the items recovered from the van. These included a dated receipt from a Pleasanton motel, which linked the suspects with the crime scene, and the gag that contained traces of Vanessa's saliva. Detectives now realized that they were holding a serial killer or killers.

A grand jury was summoned to determine whether there was sufficient evidence to commit the accused to trial. During the hearing Daveggio's 16-year-old daughter testified that on Thanksgiving Day 1997 her father had asked her if she wanted to join him in a 'hunt' for a victim.

'He told me I would never know if I'd like killing someone unless I had tried,' she said.

He had also sought her reassurance that if he did kill someone he could count on her to hide him out. The reluctant teenager was then browbeaten by Mickie Michaud, who could barely contain her excitement at the thought of kidnapping someone they would have at their mercy.

'Michelle told me [that the day after Thanksgiving] was the biggest shopping day of the year and would be the best day to go kill somebody... She tried to get me to go with her and my dad. But I wasn't going with them.'

In sentencing Daveggio and Michaud to death Judge Larry Goodman cited 'overwhelming and undisputed' evidence of their guilt. He described the murder of Vanessa Lei Samson as 'vile, cruel, senseless, depraved, brutal, evil and vicious'. His comments were echoed by Deputy District Attorney Angela Backers for the prosecution, who said that the case was unique in the annals of Alameda County, being an example of 'pure evil and utter depravity'. Michaud had described each vicious assault as an 'adventure', and Daveggio had referred to them as 'huntings'.

'These two defendants are simply the worst of the worst,' Backers declared.

Prior to the sentencing of the couple, the Samson family were allowed to address Daveggio, who remained unmoved and again denied that he had been responsible for the death of Vanessa Lei. Her mother, Christina, told the court that she cries every day for the loss of her daughter, reserving her grief for the early morning hours when the rest of the family are asleep and cannot hear her. What makes her loss all the more unbearable is knowing that her daughter was tortured and assaulted. 'She was in terror. Frightened beyond words,' Christina Samson told the court. 'She was brutally tortured and she was defenseless and alone... With the murder of my Vanessa Lei, a part of me died.'

INDEX

PICTURE CREDITS

AP Photo: 160, 163

Corbis: 31, 93, 113, 147, 154, 177

Nova Scotia Archives and Records Management: 45

Press Association: 83, 136, 192, 196

Rex Features: 87, 142, 166, 186, 212

Riverside Public Library: 24

Serial Killers TV: 181

Topfoto: 15, 61, 68, 70, 78, 106

Zuma Press: 134,170